THE INFINITE FALL

THE INFINITE FALL

A SCIENTIFIC APPROACH TO THE SECOND PILLAR OF ETERNITY

TRENT DEE STEPHENS, PhD

CFI
An imprint of Cedar Fort, Inc.
Springville, Utah

ISBN 13: 978-1-4621-3978-1

Published by CFI, an imprint of Cedar Fort, Inc.
2373 W. 700 S., Springville, UT, 84663
Distributed by Cedar Fort, Inc., www.cedarfort.com

Library of Congress Control Number: 2021931734

Cover design by Courtney Proby

Printed in the United States of America

10 9 8 7 6 5 4 3 2 1

Printed on acid-free paper

CONTENTS

INTRODUCTION

How does one reconcile the religious teaching that Adam was the first man and lived a mere 6,000 years ago; that there was no death of any life on earth before the Fall of Adam and Eve, with the scientific perspective that life has been living and dying on this planet for billions of years; and that *Homo sapiens* have been around for some 300,000 years? Most people either cling to their religious beliefs and ignore the scientific data, or ignore the religious "myths" in favor of science. Some people maintain intermediate ground where the conflict is either ignored or pushed into a closet for future consideration. As a professional biologist and an active member of The Church of Jesus Christ of Latter-day Saints, I have never been comfortable with any of those solutions and have spent much of my life attempting to reconcile those issues. The result of my lifelong investigation into some common ground where the story of the Fall of Adam and Eve, which is key to Christian belief, can be reconciled with the overwhelming scientific data is this book: *The Infinite Fall.*

A study of US young Christians published in 2016 by David Kinnaman, president of the private, for-profit research organization the Barna Group, identified six reasons "why nearly three out of every five young Christians (59%) disconnect either permanently or for an extended period of time from church life after age 15."[1] The tension between Christianity and science was listed as reason number 3, but at least five of the six reasons included some aspect of the science/religion conflict. Kinnaman found:

> Reason #1—Churches seem overprotective. . . . Much of their [young Christians'] experience of Christianity feels stifling, fear-based and risk-averse. One-quarter of 18– to 29–year-olds said "Christians demonize everything outside of the church" . . .

> Reason #2—Teens' and twentysomethings' experience of Christianity is shallow . . . church is boring . . . [and] God seems missing from [their church experience] . . .
>
> Reason #3—Churches come across as antagonistic to science . . . young adults feel . . . the tension . . . between Christianity and science . . . churches are out of step with the scientific world . . . they have "been turned off by the creation-versus-evolution debate" . . . many science-minded young Christians are struggling to find ways of staying faithful to their beliefs and to their professional calling in science-related industries.
>
> Reason #4—Young Christians' church experiences related to sexuality are often simplistic, judgmental.
>
> Reason #5—They wrestle with the exclusive nature of Christianity . . . [in which] open-mindedness, tolerance and acceptance." [appear to be missing].
>
> Reason #6—The church feels unfriendly to those who doubt. Young adults . . . do not feel safe admitting that sometimes Christianity does not make sense . . . [and] many feel that the church's response to doubt is trivial.[1]

Whereas many young members of The Church of Jesus Christ of Latter-day Saints may fall away for similar reasons, a recent study by the Pew Research Center, which has been tracking Millennials by state, has found that young members of The Church of Jesus Christ in Utah drop out at a lower rate than other Christians (36 percent versus 59 percent). However, that rate is on the rise. One reason given in a recent report was that in the information age, "transparency" and "truth" are important commodities, which many Millennials find lacking in their religious experience.[2]

In another Utah study by Jana Riess and Benjamin Knoll, "Millennials cite feeling judged or misunderstood, a distrust for church leadership, and LGBT issues as their top three reasons for leaving." "Personal views" and simply "drifted away" rounded out the top five reasons for Millennials leaving the Church of Jesus Christ.[3]

Another study of Christians in general by the Barna Group, in 2017, found that of 1,015 US adults, ages 18 and older, "Those who have been through college and encountered an array of ideas, philosophies and worldviews are twice as likely to experience doubt [about Christian beliefs] as those who have a high school education or less (37% vs. 19%)."[4]

Whereas the conflict between science and religion apparently is not as high a priority for those dropping out of the Church of Jesus Christ as for other Christians, it has been my experience in talking to college students over the years that there remains an uncomfortable stress, especially concerning Adam and the Fall versus evolution and the age of the biological world, even among young people who remain active in the Church.

In a 2013 YouTube podcast, John Dehlin listed six scientific issues for "why committed Mormons leave the Church:" age of the earth (6,000 years?), Adam and Eve, Noah's ark story (global flood), evolution, the Book of Mormon (including Native Americans having Asiatic DNA), and the book of Abraham text not matching the papyrus.[5] I have addressed most of these issues in my previous books (*Evolution and Mormonism: a Quest for Understanding*, with Jeff Meldrum and Forest Peterson, Signature, 2001; *Who Are the Children of Lehi? DNA and the Book of Mormon*, with Jeff Meldrum, Kofford Books, 2007; *The Infinite Creation: Unifying Science and Latter-day Saint Theology*, Cedar Fort, 2020). This current book also deals with some of these issues, especially Adam and Eve, the age of the earth, and evolution.

Martin Lings, an English Muslim author and philosopher, stated in 1970, "More cases of loss of religious faith are to be traced to the theory of evolution . . . than to anything else."[6] In this brief statement, Lings outlined the dilemma experienced by many Muslims, Jews, and Christians following the publication of *On the Origin of Species* by Charles Darwin in 1859. In our ever more complex world, fifty years after Lings' statement, there may be many other reasons for loss of religious faith, but the conflict between science and religion is still among the leading causes.

In his impactful book *The Outline of History*, H. G. Wells stated concerning the impact of Darwin's theory of evolution by natural selection on the history of mankind:

> It was only slowly that the general intelligence of the Western world was awakened to two disconcerting facts: firstly, that the succession of life in the geological record did not correspond to the acts of the six days of creation; and, secondly, that the record, in harmony with a mass of biological facts, pointed away from the Bible assertion of a separate creation of each species straight towards a genetic relation between all

> forms of life, in which even man was included!... If all the animals and man had been evolved in this ascendant manner, then there had been no first parents, no Eden, and no Fall. And if there had been no fall, then the entire historical fabric of Christianity, the story of the first sin and the reason for an atonement, upon which the current teaching based Christian emotion and morality, collapsed like a house of cards.
>
> It was with something like horror, therefore, that great numbers of honest and religious-spirited men followed the work of the great English naturalist, Charles Darwin.[7]

But what is this "historical fabric of Christianity" to which Wells refers? In their marvelous recent book, *The Christ Who Heals*, Fiona and Terryl Givens describe some key differences between the theology of the Fall and Atonement of The Church of Jesus Christ of Latter-day Saints and that of other Christian churches:

> For the unfailing plan initiated in heavenly councils that foresaw a necessary immersion in mortal experience, a Christianity stripped of premortal existence becomes instead a story that is primarily about recuperation, repair, and rehabilitation. The loss of this truth about pre-earthly councils and covenants acted as a falling domino that set in motion an entire series of catastrophic changes to the Christian understanding of God, humans, and Christ's role in our redemption.[8]

It was this "Christianity stripped of premortal existence" that viewed with horror the truths of geology and biology being revealed in the nineteenth and later centuries. Only with an understanding of those premortal heavenly councils and the truly infinite nature of the Fall can we begin to reconcile the truths concerning our place in heaven and nature. It is my opinion that members of the Church of Jesus Christ who fall away over issues of science versus religion often fail to appreciate this important difference between our theology and that of "mainstream" Christianity. I highly recommend the Givens' book as an in-depth historical account of this difference.

In a speech given at BYU in 1981, Elder Bruce R. McConkie, of the Quorum of the Twelve Apostles, described what he called the three pillars of eternity:

> I pray that we may receive a mighty outpouring of that Spirit as we consider the three pillars of eternity—the three great eternal verities upon which salvation rests.

> My purpose is to take the three greatest events that have ever occurred in all eternity and show how they are interwoven to form one grand plan of salvation.
>
> If we can gain an understanding of them, then the whole eternal scheme of things will fall into place, and we will be in a position to work out our salvation. If we do not build our house of salvation on a true foundation, we will never make the spiritual progress that will prepare us to enter the Eternal Presence.
>
> The three pillars of eternity, the three events, preeminent and transcendent above all others, are the creation, the fall, and the atonement. These three are the foundations upon which all things rest. Without any one of them all things would lose their purpose and meaning, and the plans and designs of Deity would come to naught.[9]

With these three pillars of eternity, Elder McConkie, simply and eloquently outlined the entirety of the great plan of happiness and the foundation of our faith.

In a 1991 *Ensign* article, Russell M. Nelson, then an apostle, stated,

> In a very real way, the atonement of Jesus Christ affects each of our lives and the life of every human being who ever lived. Understanding the significance of His atonement is fundamental to choices we make in all facets of our lives. The atonement of the Lord is central to our faith.
>
> We are scripturally bound to study it and to teach it. . . .
>
> But before one can comprehend the *atonement* of Christ, one must first understand the *fall* of Adam. And before one can comprehend the fall of Adam, one must first understand the *Creation.* These three pillars of eternity relate to one another.[10]

Concerning the eternal Atonement, Amulek stated, "It must be an infinite and eternal sacrifice."[11] We also read in Doctrine and Covenants 20:17, "By these things we know that there is a God in heaven, who is infinite and eternal, from everlasting to everlasting the same unchangeable God, the framer of heaven and earth, and all things which are in them." These scriptures imply that the terms "eternal" and "infinite" are more-or-less equivalent. Both Jacob and Nephi referred to the "infinite atonement."[12] Thus, the three pillars of eternity may also be described as the "three pillars of infinity." The first pillar, then, can be called the *infinite Creation*, the second the *infinite Fall*, and the third the *infinite Atonement.*

In his book *The Infinite Atonement*, Elder Tad Callister described the infinite nature of the Atonement by stating: "The phrase 'infinite atonement' or 'infinite sacrifice' may refer to an atonement or sacrifice by a God, a being who is infinite in knowledge, power, and glory. . . . Accordingly, the Atonement is 'infinite' because its source is 'infinite.'"[13]

Likewise, it may also be said that the phrase "infinite fall" refers to a fall orchestrated by a God, a being who is infinite in knowledge, power, and glory. Accordingly, the Creation, the Fall, and the Atonement are all "infinite" because they all have their source in the "infinite."

Elder Callister stated in his book, "An attempt to master this doctrine requires an immersion of all our senses, all our feelings, and all our intellect. . . . The Atonement is not a doctrine that lends itself to some singular approach"[11] Intellectually, the *infinite* is not a simple concept. It requires every ounce of effort and intellectual energy we can muster. Our understanding of the *infinite* nature of the *Fall*, however, will allow us to reconcile what has been revealed through ancient and modern prophets, and what has been revealed through modern science. Reconciling what we know about the Fall from science and the scriptures is critical to our eternal progression, because understanding these infinite pillars "is fundamental to choices we make in all facets of our lives."[9]

Young people in the Church of Jesus Christ are constantly making fundamental choices in their lives. Some of those choices are made by pitting information they are given from religion against information they are given from science. Many Church leaders have admonished the youth that making such distinction is not necessary. I fully and heartily agree, but young people are often left without a clear path to reconciliation. One of the main reasons for this deficiency is that the path to scientific and religious reconciliation is not a simple one, but one which requires considerable intellectual rigor.

To paraphrase Elder Callister, *infinity* itself must be pondered, analyzed, and internalized. It is, by its very nature, the most supernal, mind-expanding, passionate concept the universe has ever known. Furthermore, understanding that the Fall is *infinite* allows us to move the implications of the Fall out of a strictly temporal context into an *infinite* context, where the actual *time* of the Fall in human history becomes irrelevant. Once this concept of *infinity* is applied to the Fall, the apparent conflicts between science and religion over this critical event will evaporate.

We may still say that we "see through a glass darkly."[14] Nonetheless, glass has changed considerably since Paul coined that line in the mid-first century AD. His glass was very small, very expensive, very rare, and not at all transparent. Today, we can create entire buildings of perfectly smooth, perfectly transparent, and relatively inexpensive plate glass. Today, we live way beyond Paul's wildest imagination. Our knowledge of science and the scriptures is vastly greater than Paul's. Paul knew nothing of the physiology of respiration or digestion. Fossils were either unheard of or were completely misunderstood and misrepresented. The earth was the center of a very small universe, and geological time had almost no meaning whatsoever.

The Infinite Fall employs not only the scriptures and the words of modern prophets, but it also includes knowledge revealed by modern science. There are many paradigms associated with our understanding of the Fall—many stories that have been handed down through the ages. The irony of the conflict these stories create between what we *think* we understand about the Fall and what we have learned from modern science is that much of what we think we know about the Fall is *not even found in the scriptures*. If the perceived conflict between the Fall and modern science is based upon paradigms that have no scriptural basis, maybe it's time to reconsider those unfounded paradigms and cut them loose.

NOTES

1. David Kinnaman, "You Lost Me: Why Young Christians Are Leaving Church . . . and Rethinking Faith, Baker Books," Reprint edition, Ada, MI, 2016; barna.com/research/six-reasons-young-christians-leave-church.
2. Heidi Hatch, "Losing their religion: Millennials, including Utahns, leaving church," KUTV, Tuesday, May 9th 2017, kutv.com/news/local/losing-their-religion-millennials-including-utahns-leaving-church.
3. Karissa Neely, "Millennials and why they leave The Church of Jesus Christ of Latter-day Saints," *Daily Herald*, Apr. 2, 2019, heraldextra.com/special-section/lds/spring2019/millennials-and-why-they-leave-the-church-of-jesus-christ/article_90b19e13–6259–572d-b6e3–8c2f-60c8dada.html.

4. barna.com/research/two-thirds-christians-face-doubt
5. John Dehlin, "Top 5 Myths and Truths about Why Committed Mormons Leave the Church," Feb 8, 2013, youtube.com/watch?v=EP3G-JeYIN3s, retrieved 20 June 2020.
6. Martin Lings, "Signs of the Times," in *Studies in Comparative Religion*, vol 4, (1), Francis Clive-Ross, ed., (Bedfont, UK, now World Wisdom, Inc., Bloomington, IN, 1970).
7. H.G. Wells, *The outline of history—being a plain history of life and mankind* (New York: MacMillan, 1920), 416. Project Gutenberg e-book.
8. Fiona and Terryl Givens, *The Christ Who Heals, How God Restored the Truth that Saves Us* (Salt Lake City: Deseret Book, 2017).
9. McConkie, Bruce R, BYU Speeches, Feb 17, 1981.
10. Russell M. Nelson, "Standards of the Lord's Standard-Bearers," *Ensign,* Aug. 1991, 5–6; italics in original
11. Alma 34:10
12. 2 Nephi 9:7; 2 Nephi 25:16
13. Tad R. Callister, *The Infinite Atonement* (Salt Lake City: Deseret Book, 2000).
14. 1 Corinthians 13:12

CHAPTER 1

WHY IS THE FALL INFINITE?

In his 1981 BYU speech, Elder Bruce R. McConkie, said, "The three greatest events that have ever occurred in all eternity . . . the three pillars of eternity . . . the creation, the fall, and the atonement [are eternally] interwoven to form one grand plan of salvation."[1] President Russell M. Nelson has stated, "Before one can comprehend the *atonement* of Christ, one must first understand the *fall* of Adam."[2] The Fall, then, being one of the three pillars of eternity, is, in itself, eternal and infinite.

The concept of an infinite atonement and, by extension, an infinite fall, means that neither the Fall nor the Atonement is limited in space or time. Of course we know that the Atonement occurred over a three-day period a little less than two thousand years ago (April 4–6, around 33 AD). Although the Atonement itself occurred at a specific, *finite* date, its effect is infinite—being both retroactive as well as proactive. We also believe that the Fall occurred some six thousand years ago—again, at a specific, *finite* date. Nonetheless, although the date of the Fall is finite, if the influence of the Atonement is infinite, by logical extension, the infinite fall must also be unconfined by space and time—therefore, being infinite, it must be retroactive as well as proactive.

If time is viewed only mathematically as an infinitely long line, any division of that line, such as one's lifetime, is meaningless (∞/x is undefined). But with God, time is not an infinitely long line; *it doesn't exist at all.* We are told in the scriptures that "time only is measured unto men."[3] Furthermore, we are told that there was a "beginning of time"[4] and that there is a "time of the end."[5] Therefore, there is a beginning and an end to earth's existence and our sojourn here, which are measured by time. Before this time and after this time, there is no time in the infinite perspective.

To us mortals who exist during that temporal interval between the beginning of time and the end of time, the events occurring during this finite interlude are real and meaningful. The covenants we make and the ordinances we perform here, although finite in occurrence, are infinite in effect. For example, our own baptisms and sealings are proactive into the infinite future. But our baptisms and sealings for our deceased family members are retroactive to include them in that infinite future. Likewise, Christ's Atonement was both proactive for those living and yet to be born as well as retroactive for those who had died before His resurrection. In the same manner, the Fall not only affected those born after Adam and Eve were cast out of the Garden of Eden, but also the millions of people who had lived before Adam and Eve were placed into the Garden. To God, and to His children, the Fall was no more constrained in its infinite nature than was the Atonement. The infinite nature of the Fall was possible because each person born on this earth, no matter when, attended the premortal, infinite grand council in heaven where the entire plan of happiness, including the Creation, the Fall, and the Atonement, were presented and accepted.

We are told that for God "all things are present before mine eyes"[6] and that God "is the same yesterday, today, and forever; and the way is prepared for all men from the foundation of the world, if it so be that they repent and come unto him. For he that diligently seeketh shall find; and the mysteries of God shall be unfolded unto them, by the power of the Holy Ghost, as well in these times as in times of old, and as well in times of old as in times to come; wherefore, the course of the Lord is one eternal round."[7]

In his book *The Infinite Atonement*, Elder Tad Callister said, "The phrase 'infinite atonement' or 'infinite sacrifice' may refer to an atonement or sacrifice by a God, a being who is infinite in knowledge, power, and glory. . . . Accordingly, the Atonement is 'infinite' because its source is 'infinite.'"[8]

Likewise, it may also be said that the phrase "infinite fall" refers to a fall orchestrated by a God, a being who is infinite in knowledge, power, and glory. Accordingly, the Fall is "infinite" because it had its source in the "infinite."

NOTES

1. Bruce R. McConkie, BYU Speeches, Feb. 17, 1981.
2. Russell M. Nelson, "Standards of the Lord's Standard-Bearers," *Ensign,* 5–6; italics in original.
3. Alma 40:8
4. Abraham 1:3
5. Jacob 5:62; Daniel 12:9
6. Doctrine and Covenants 38:1–3
7. 1 Nephi 10:18–19
8. Tad R. Callister, *The Infinite Atonement* (Salt Lake City: Deseret Book, 2000).

CHAPTER 2

THE GREAT PLAN OF HAPPINESS

In the April 2017 general conference, Elder Weatherford T. Clayton, of the Seventy, said,

> The journey our Father prepared for us is called the plan of salvation or the plan of happiness.[1] In a grand premortal council, our Father told us about His plan.[2] When we understood it, we were so happy that we shouted for joy, and "the morning stars sang together."[3] That plan is built upon three grand pillars: the pillars of eternity.[2] The first pillar is the Creation of the earth, the setting for our mortal journey.[4, 5]
>
> The second pillar is the Fall of our first earthly parents, Adam and Eve. Because of the Fall, some marvelous things were given to us. We were able to be born and receive a physical body."[6]
>
> Knowing that we would not always choose well—or in other words, sin—Father gave us the third pillar: the Savior Jesus Christ and His Atonement. Through His suffering, Christ paid the price for both physical death and sin.[5]

Most members of The Church of Jesus Christ of Latter-day Saints are quite familiar with this third part of the story of the grand council. We are told in Abraham, "And the Lord said: Whom shall I send? And one answered like unto the Son of Man: Here am I, send me. And another answered and said: Here am I, send me. And the Lord said: I will send the first. And the second was angry, and kept not his first estate; and, at that day, many followed after him."[7]

Once God had announced that He would send His Beloved and Chosen Firstborn to be His Only Begotten Beloved Son, we each had the choice to accept or reject the plan. But in order for this third part of the plan, this third pillar, to make any sense, we were also told of and accepted the other two parts of the plan. The scriptures are clear that we were informed of the first pillar, the Creation: "And there stood one among them that was like unto God, and he said unto those who were with him: We will go down, for there is space there, and we will take of these materials, and we will make an earth whereon these may dwell; And we will prove them herewith, to see if they will do all things whatsoever the Lord their God shall command them."[8]

However, the scriptures describing the premortal world appear to be mute concerning the second pillar, the Fall. Nonetheless, in accepting the great plan of salvation, we all must have accepted Adam's part in the plan as well as Christ's part. In a sermon given in Washington, DC, on February 5, 1840, as recorded by Matthew Davis, a New York City newspaper correspondent, the Prophet Joseph Smith taught, "He [God] reigns over all things in heaven and on earth. . . . He foreordained the fall of man, but all-merciful as He is, He foreordained at the same time a plan of redemption for all mankind."[9] We are told that Adam was "called and prepared from the foundation of the world."[10] Without a fall there was no need of a redemption. "As in Adam all die, even so in Christ shall all be made alive."[11] We are all partakers of the "flesh and blood" given us by Adam,[12] just as we are all partakers of Christ's redemption.[13] Paul stated in his letter to the Romans,

> Wherefore, as by one man sin entered into the world, and death by sin; and so death passed upon all men, for that all have sinned: . . . Therefore as by the offence of one judgment came upon all men to condemnation; even so by the righteousness of one the free gift came upon all men unto justification of life. For as by one man's disobedience many were made sinners, so by obedience of one shall many be made righteous.[14]

Jacob described the infinite nature of the Atonement:

> For as death hath passed upon all men, to fulfil the merciful plan of the great Creator, there must needs be a power of resurrection, and the resurrection must needs come unto man by reason of the fall; and the fall came by reason of transgression; and because man became

> fallen they were cut off from the presence of the Lord. Wherefore, it must needs be an infinite atonement—save it should be an infinite atonement this corruption could not put on incorruption. Wherefore, the first judgment which came upon man must needs have remained to an endless duration.[15]

Jacob stated that first, "death hath passed upon all men, to fulfil the merciful plan of the great Creator." Second, "the resurrection must needs come unto man by reason of the fall." Third, the Atonement "must needs be an infinite atonement." Had it not been infinite, "the first judgment which came upon man must needs have remained to an endless duration." Furthermore, "the bodies and the spirits of men will be restored one to the other; and it is by the power of the resurrection of the Holy One of Israel . . . and all men become incorruptible, and immortal, and they are living souls, having a perfect knowledge like unto us in the flesh, save it be that our knowledge shall be perfect."[16] In the previous two paragraphs, the parallel between the Fall and the Atonement has been emphasized in the scriptures: "As in Adam all die, even so in Christ shall all be made alive."[11] Jacob pointed out that the Atonement was an infinite atonement affecting ALL men. He also stated that the Fall passed upon ALL men.[14] The Fall is an infinite fall, for "the first judgment which came upon man must needs have remained to an *endless duration*."[15]

Jacob stated that as a result of the Fall, we are all "cut off from the presence of the Lord."[15] As each child leaves the premortal state to come to earth, he or she is cut off from the presence of the Lord at that point. In order for God's justice to be a righteous justice, that decision to leave God's presence must be based on our own agency. We cannot be forced from God's presence; we must leave of our own will. Furthermore, by the same reasoning, we must have accepted the mechanism by which our separation from God came about (the Fall). Without our agreement to the Fall, we would have become partakers of an unrighteous judgement against our agency.

We are well aware that the Atonement and Resurrection did not just affect those born after Christ's death and resurrection. At the time of Christ's resurrection, we are told that "the graves were opened; and many bodies of the saints which slept arose."[17] Therefore, Christ's resurrection was *infinite* in affecting ALL humans, even affecting those humans born before Him. Therefore, those who lived and died many generations before Christ, as well as those who have lived for generations after the Atonement, agreed in the grand premortal council to the *infinite Atonement.*

Within infinity, time does not exist. We are told in the scriptures that "time only is measured unto men."[18] Modern science is on the same page with the scriptures. As part of quantum mechanics, Albert Einstein demonstrated that time is not absolute but relative. He stated, "Time is simply a human construct and does not even exist outside our minds."[19]

Furthermore, we are told that there was a "beginning of time."[20] So the council in heaven transpired during that infinite period *before* the beginning of time. Therefore, as with the infinite atonement, the infinite fall was timeless. Therefore, from an infinite fall perspective, Adam and Eve did not have to be temporally the first people on earth for their fall to be valid and affect ALL people born on earth—as we ALL agreed to be partakers in the Fall while we were yet residing in an infinite, immortal state.

We are told in the scriptures "that this is the man who receiveth salvation, through the atonement which was prepared from the foundation of the world for all mankind, which ever were since the fall of Adam, or who are, or who ever shall be, even unto the end of the world."[21] We are also informed that death fulfilled "the merciful plan of the great Creator."[22]

Just as Christ was the first fruits and was chosen in the great council in heaven before the foundations of the world, so too was Adam chosen in the same council as the first man. We don't seem to have much trouble understanding that the term "first fruits" is a metaphor not to be taken literally, but the term "first man" apparently has caused a rift between science and religion for a long time. Perhaps the name "first man" in the scriptures is intended as a title rather than a statement of his position in the temporal line of humanity. We commonly use the term "first" as a title: "First Presidency," "first knight," the greatest knight at the time; "first boy," the head student at a school; "first lieutenant," the senior lieutenant; "First Lady," the wife of the president. We understand perfectly well that those titles are not intended to have any chronological intent. Likewise, when Adam was chosen as the "first man," we were in a grand council in an *immortal, timeless* state. Adam represents ALL humanity in the Fall. In order for us to be tested it was necessary for us to leave God's presence—thus the Fall—and then return to His presence—thus the Atonement. We left the presence of God when we came to earth, and our objective in life is to return to God's presence. "Yea, behold, this death bringeth to pass the resurrection, and redeemeth all mankind from the first death—that spiritual death; for all mankind, by the fall of Adam being cut off from the presence of the Lord, are considered as dead, both as to things temporal and to things spiritual. But behold, the resurrection of Christ redeemeth mankind, yea, even all mankind, and bringeth them back into the presence of the Lord."[23]

We are told in Mosiah, "For behold, and also his blood atoneth for the sins of those who have fallen by the transgression of Adam, who have died not knowing the will of God concerning them, or who have ignorantly sinned. And even if it were possible that little children could sin they could not be saved; but I say unto you they are blessed; for behold, as in Adam, or by nature, they fall, even so the blood of Christ atoneth for their sins."[24] We know that this blessing extends to millions of people born before and after the time of Jesus Christ, many of whom have never even heard His name. It is also reasonable to assume that such blessings also extend to those born before Adam—who never even heard *his* name during their mortality.

We all accepted the great plan of happiness in the premortal world, both the part Jesus Christ was to play in the Atonement, which is well documented in the scriptures, and the part Adam was to play in the Fall, which is implied in the scriptures and addressed by modern prophets.[25] Did it make any difference when these two eternal events actually occurred? We know that the Atonement affected people who lived before Christ as well as those who lived after Him. The presence of people on the earth before Christ's birth is indisputable. Adam's place in the earth's chronology is a different matter. For millennia, the descendants of the Abrahamic covenant—Jews, Christians, and Muslims—have believed that *all* human beings descended from Adam and were born *after* the Fall, only some six thousand years ago. The presence of any humans on earth before Adam has been flatly denied by the Abrahamic religions until very recent times.

The concept that Earth's entire history spanned only six thousand years was simply taken for granted and not even questioned until about two hundred years ago. Furthermore, the concept of three eternal pillars, including the infinite fall, were not explicitly part of our, or anyone's, theology until about forty years ago.[26] Only very recently have the full eternal implications of the eternal fall been addressed by our living prophets.[25]

In 1830 to 1833, Charles Lyell published his multi-volume *Principles of Geology*,[27] which demonstrated that the earth was much older than anyone had previously suspected. DNA analysis suggests that the first anatomically modern human, *Homo sapiens*, emerged as a separate species some 315,000 years ago.[28] Fossil remains and stone tools from *Homo sapiens* living 300,000 years ago were discovered in 2017 at Jebel Irhoud, Morocco.[27] The stunning cave paintings in France, such as those of the Lascaux Cave complex, were discovered in 1940, providing indisputable evidence that artistic humans lived on earth at least 20,000 years before Adam and Eve.[29] Breathtaking paintings in Chauvet Cave,[30] dating from around 30,000 to 35,000 years ago, discovered in 1994, didn't have to be dated by their artists—they were dated by time itself. More than eighty separate radio carbon studies have been conducted from torch marks on the ceiling, from the paintings themselves, and from charcoal and animal bones on the cave floor.[31]

For God, there is no temporal difference between the finite, mortal world and the infinite spirit world. The Fall, therefore, applies to the world of spirits as well as the world of mortals. It matters not at all when, in the course of earth's history, Adam came to earth. With God, there is no time. All humans are partakers of the Fall just as much as we are partakers of the Atonement, because we accepted both in the grand council in heaven before the foundations of the earth were ever laid and before the beginning of time, "as well in these times as in times of old, and as well in times of old as in times to come; wherefore, the course of the Lord is one eternal round."[32]

Enos has told us,

> And there came a voice unto me, saying: Enos, thy sins are forgiven thee, and thou shalt be blessed. And I, Enos, knew that God could not lie; wherefore, my guilt was swept away. And I said: Lord, how is it done? And he said unto me: Because of thy faith in Christ,

> whom thou hast never before heard nor seen. And many years pass away before he shall manifest himself in the flesh; wherefore, go to, thy faith hath made thee whole.[33]

God did not say to Enos, "Thy sins *will be* forgiven thee *after* Christ has paid the price." He said, "Thy sins *are* forgiven thee." He said, "Go to, thy faith *hath* made thee whole." The Atonement would not occur for another 450 years, yet to God, it was as if it had already occurred. We might also consider that the artists who decorated the Chauvet Cave and the Lascaux Cave complex, over 20,000 years before Adam and Eve, were partakers of the Fall *as if it had already occurred.*

If, according to Albert Einstein, the "distinction between past, present, and future is only an illusion,"[19] then the concept that Adam was chronologically the "first man," who lived some 6,000 years ago, before any other human being, or even animals, for that matter, is also an illusion. If we simply understand that "first man" is a title, a well-deserved title for Adam, then most of the artificial controversy that has existed for years between science and religion simply vanishes. The revelation that time is an illusion does not mean that Adam was mythical or that the Fall was irrelevant. Indeed I agree with Elder Bruce R. McConkie[26] that the Fall of Adam is one of the three pillars of our faith, one of the three most important events in all of human history, upon which the gospel of Jesus Christ is founded.

In the priesthood session of the April 2016 general conference, President Henry B. Eyring, of the First Presidency, stated,

> Before we were born we lived in a family with our exalted and eternal Heavenly Father. He ordained a plan [in the grand council] that enables us to advance and progress to become like him. . . . The purpose of the plan was to allow us the privilege of living forever as our Heavenly Father lives. This gospel plan offered us a life of mortality in which we would be tested [the Fall]. A promise was given, that through the Atonement of Jesus Christ, if we obey the laws and priesthood ordinances of the Gospel, we would have eternal life, the greatest of all His gifts.[34]

We all were foreordained before we came to earth that we would accept Jesus Christ as our Savior.

> And we know that all things work together for good to them that love God, to them who are the called according to his purpose. For whom he did foreknow, he also did predestinate to be conformed to the image of his Son, that he might be the firstborn among many brethren. Moreover whom he did predestinate, them he also called: and whom he called, them he also justified: and whom he justified, them he also glorified.[35]

> According as he hath chosen us in him before the foundation of the world, that we should be holy and without blame before him in love.[36]

All of us who hold the priesthood and/or hold specific callings in the Church were foreordained to those callings as well before we came to earth. The following scriptures explain this concept:

> And those priests were ordained after the order of his Son . . . being called and prepared from the foundation of the world according to the foreknowledge of God, on account of their exceeding faith and good works.[37]

> Before I formed thee in the belly I knew thee; and before thou camest forth out of the womb I sanctified thee, and I ordained thee a prophet unto the nations.[38]

> And God saw these souls that they were good, and he stood in the midst of them, and he said: These I will make my rulers; for he stood among those that were spirits, and he saw that they were good; and he said unto me: Abraham, thou art one of them; thou wast chosen before thou wast born.[39]

We apparently all attended the grand council, and two-thirds of us, the host of heaven, marveled at the great plan of our God[40] and shouted for joy at its prospect.[41] At that council, Satan, who was from the beginning, "came before . . . [God], saying—Behold, here am I, send me, I will be thy son, and I will redeem all mankind, that one soul shall not be lost, and surely I will do it; wherefore give me thine honor."[42] Then God's "Beloved, which was my Beloved and Chosen from the beginning, said unto me—Father, thy will be done, and the glory be thine forever."[43]

Abraham gave a somewhat more detailed, more poetic account of the grand council:

> And there stood one among them that was like unto God, and he said unto those who were with him: We will go down, for there is space there, and we will take of these materials, and we will make an earth whereon these may dwell; And we will prove them herewith, to see if they will do all things whatsoever the Lord their God shall command them; And they who keep their first estate shall be added upon; and they who keep not their first estate shall not have glory in the same kingdom with those who keep their first estate; and they who keep their second estate shall have glory added upon their heads for ever and ever. And the Lord said: Whom shall I send? And one answered like unto the Son of Man: Here am I, send me. And another answered and said: Here am I, send me. And the Lord said: I will send the first. And the second was angry, and kept not his first estate; and, at that day, many followed after him.[44]

Satan, in his anger, initiated a war in heaven during which he drew away one-third of heaven's host. The casting out of Satan and his host is poetically described in the book of Revelation: "And there was war in heaven: Michael and his angels fought against the dragon; and the dragon fought and his angels. . . . And his tail drew the third part of the stars of heaven, and did cast them to the earth."[45] The story is also told in modern revelation: "The devil . . . rebelled against me, saying, Give me thine honor, which is my power; and also a third part of the hosts of heaven turned he away from me because of their agency."[46]

It may be that, in some way through being cast out of heaven, Satan didn't fully understand the great plan of happiness or Adam and Eve's part in it, for we read in Moses, "And Satan put it into the heart of the serpent, (for he had drawn away many after him,) and he sought also to beguile Eve, for he knew not the mind of God, wherefore he sought to destroy the world."[47]

Satan may have been surprised by the Fall and its consequences, but God and Christ certainly were not. Many Christians seem to believe that God was taken by surprise by Adam's disobedience in the Garden of Eden and had to *then* devise a plan to save us. Such belief flies in the face of the notion that God is omniscient. Not only was Adam and Eve's behavior in the Garden not surprising to God, but it was also part of the great plan, as presented to us in the grand council. Lehi, in his blessing to Jacob, taught,

> If Adam had not transgressed he would not have fallen, but he would have remained in the garden of Eden. And all things which were created must have remained in the same state in which they were after they were created; and they must have remained forever, and had no end. And they would have had no children; wherefore they would have remained in a state of innocence, having no joy, for they knew no misery; doing no good, for they knew no sin. But behold, all things have been done in the wisdom of him who knoweth all things. Adam fell that men might be; and men are, that they might have joy.[48]

As will be discussed in detail in a later chapter, the "all things" and "they" stated in this scripture must refer specifically to Adam and Eve and their condition in the Garden before the Fall—for they were the only "things" that could know sin.

NOTES

1. Alma 42:8
2. Abraham 3:24–28
3. Job 38:7
4. 3 Nephi 9:15
5. Weatherford T. Clayton, "Our Father's Glorious Plan," April 2017 general conference.
6. 2 Nephi 2:22–25
7. Abraham 3:27–28
8. Abraham 3:24–25
9. Richard L. Bushman, *Joseph Smith: Rough Stone Rolling*, 394–395; The Church of Jesus Christ of Latter-day Saints, *Saints: The Story of the Church of Jesus Christ in the Latter Days*, vol. 1, The Standard of Truth: 1815–1846, 411, The Church of Jesus Christ of Latter-day Saints, 2018. See also Mathew L. Davis to Mrs. Matthew [Mary] L. Davis, Feb. 6, 1840, Church History Library.
10. Alma 13:3
11. 1 Corinthians 15:22
12. Hebrews 2:14
13. Hebrews 3:14
14. Romans 5:12–19
15. 2 Nephi 9:6–7; italics added
16. 2 Nephi 9:12–13
17. Matthew 27: 52
18. Alma 40:8
19. *The New Quotable Einstein*, Alice Calaprice, ed. (Princeton University Press, 2005).

20. Abraham 1:3
21. Mosiah 4:7; see also Alma 12:33 and 22:13
22. 2 Nephi 9:6
23. Helaman 14:16–17
24. Mosiah 3:11, 16
25. Russell M. Nelson, "Standards of the Lord's Standard-Bearers," *Ensign,* Aug. 1991, 5–6; italics in original.
26. Bruce R. McConkie, BYU Speeches, Feb 17, 1981.
27. Roy S. Porter, "Charles Lyell and the Principles of the History of Geology," *The British Journal for the History of Science,* 1976, 32:91–103.
28. Ewan Callaway, "Oldest Homo sapiens fossil claim rewrites our species' history," *Nature,* doi: 10.1038/nature.2017.22114, June 7, 2017.
29. Gergory Curtis, *The Cave Painters: Probing the Mysteries of the World's First Artists,* (New York, Knopf, 2006).
30. Jean-Marie Chauvet et al., *Dawn of Art: The Chauvet Cave*, English translation by Paul G. Bahn from the French edition *La Grotte Chauvet*, New York: Harry Abram, NY, 1996
31. Zach Zorich, "A Chauvet Primer," *Archaeology*, 64*:39,* March–April 2011.
32. 1 Nephi 10:18–19
33. Enos 1:5–8
34. Henry B. Eyring, "Eternal Families," April 2016 general conference.
35. Romans 8:28–30
36. Ephesians 1:4
37. Alma 13:3
38. Jeremiah 1:5
39. Abraham 3:22
40. 2 Nephi 9:13
41. Job 38:7
42. Moses 4:1
43. Moses 4:2
44. Abraham 3:24–28
45. Revelation 12:7 and 12:4
46. Doctrine and Covenants 29:36
47. Moses 4:6
48. 2 Nephi 2:22–25

CHAPTER 3

ADAM AND EVE'S PLACE IN INFINITY

We have learned through modern revelation that Adam's premortal and postmortal name is Michael the Archangel. These three concepts—that Adam had a premortal existence, that he was Michael in that existence, and that he continued as Michael in his postmortal existence—are key to understanding who Adam is and how truly powerful he is as an infinite, immortal being. The term "archangel" is derived from the Greek word ἀρχάγγελος, meaning chief angel, principal angel, or "angel of origin," which may also be interpreted as "first angel."

Michael's name shows up nine times in the Doctrine and Covenants. The first mention is part of that marvelous revelation concerning Christ's Second Coming as recorded in section 27:

> The hour cometh that I will drink of the fruit of the vine with you on the earth, and with Moroni, . . . Elias, . . . John [the Baptist], . . . Elijah, . . . Joseph and Jacob, and Isaac, and Abraham, . . . Peter, and James, and John.[1]
>
> "And also with Michael, or Adam, the father of all, the prince of all, the ancient of days.[2]
>
> And also with all those whom my Father hath given me out of the world.[3]

Second, we are told in Doctrine and Covenants 29 that Michael, Adam, will participate in the Resurrection: "But, behold, verily I say unto you, before the earth shall pass away, Michael, mine archangel, shall sound his trump, and then shall all the dead awake, for their graves shall be opened, and they shall come forth—yea, even all."[4]

Thus, Michael—Adam, the first angel, the first man—will be a major player in the Resurrection, the result of the Atonement. First Thessalonians 4:16 refers to the same event, although in a more obscure manner: "For the Lord himself shall descend from heaven with a shout, with the voice of the archangel, and with the trump of God: and the dead in Christ shall rise first."

Third, we read in Doctrine and Covenants 78 that the Lord God "hath appointed Michael your prince, and established his feet, and set him upon high, and given unto him the keys of salvation under the counsel and direction of the Holy One, who is without beginning of days or end of life."[5]

So, Adam, the facilitator of the Fall, is described here as having "the keys of salvation." The fourth through seventh references are in Doctrine and Covenants section 88:

> The seventh angel [Michael] shall sound his trump; and he shall stand forth upon the land and upon the sea, and swear in the name of him who sitteth upon the throne, that there shall be time no longer; and Satan shall be bound, that old serpent, who is called the devil, and shall not be loosed for the space of a thousand years. And then he shall be loosed for a little season, that he may gather together his armies.[6]

This verse tells us that Michael, Adam, is in charge of time—at least the end time. We are further told in Doctrine and Covenants 88 that the great war between good and evil, which began in the premortal world (see Revelation 12:7, as discussed below), will resume at the end of the world.

> And Michael, the seventh angel, even the archangel, shall gather together his armies, even the hosts of heaven. And the devil shall gather together his armies; even the hosts of hell, and shall come up to battle against Michael and his armies. For Michael shall fight their battles, and shall overcome him who seeketh the throne of him who sitteth upon the throne, even the Lamb.[7]

Michael is not only the first angel but also the seventh, the last angel. Eighth, we are instructed in Doctrine and Covenants 107:

> Three years previous to the death of Adam, he called Seth, Enos, Cainan, Mahalaleel, Jared, Enoch, and Methuselah, who were all high priests, with the residue of his posterity who were righteous, into the valley of Adam-ondi-Ahman, and there bestowed upon them his last blessing. And the Lord appeared unto them, and they rose up and blessed Adam, and called him Michael, the prince, the archangel.[8]

Ninth, in Doctrine and Covenants 128, Michael is praised along with many others in Joseph Smith's poetic tribute to the Restoration.

> Now, what do we hear in the gospel which we have received? A voice of gladness! A voice of mercy from heaven; and a voice of truth out of the earth; glad tidings for the dead; a voice of gladness for the living and the dead; glad tidings of great joy. How beautiful upon the mountains are the feet of those that bring glad tidings of good things, and that say unto Zion: Behold, thy God reigneth! As the dews of Carmel, so shall the knowledge of God descend upon them!
>
> And again, what do we hear? Glad tidings from Cumorah! Moroni, an angel from heaven, declaring the fulfilment of the prophets—the book to be revealed. A voice of the Lord in the wilderness of Fayette, Seneca county, declaring the three witnesses to bear record of the book! The voice of Michael on the banks of the Susquehanna, detecting the devil when he appeared as an angel of light! The voice of Peter, James, and John in the wilderness between Harmony, Susquehanna county, and Colesville, Broome county, on the Susquehanna river, declaring themselves as possessing the keys of the kingdom, and of the dispensation of the fulness of times!
>
> And again, the voice of God in the chamber of old Father Whitmer, in Fayette, Seneca county, and at sundry times, and in divers places through all the travels and tribulations of this Church of Jesus Christ of Latter-day Saints! And the voice of Michael, the archangel; the voice of Gabriel, and of Raphael, and of divers angels, from Michael or Adam down to the present time, all declaring their dispensation, their rights, their keys, their honors, their majesty and glory, and the power of their priesthood; giving line upon line, precept upon precept; here a little, and there a little; giving us consolation by holding forth that which is to come, confirming our hope![9]

Alonzo Gaskill discussed this incident when "on the banks of the Susquehanna, [Michael detected] . . . the devil when he appeared as an angel of light!" He stated, "One contemporary of Joseph and Oliver [one Addison Everett] said that he heard the Prophet say that this Satanic appearance happened as these two brethren were running from a mob. It is conjectured by this same source that in their frightened and exhausted state, Lucifer tried to deceive them by giving them a false revelation."[10] It is interesting here that Gaskill did not mention Michael's intervention in the incident, but went on to discuss how to detect the devil when he appears as an angel of light as recorded in Doctrine and Covenants 129:8. If we literally read between the lines of sections 128 and 129, it appears that it was Michael who taught Joseph this principle. Such intervention makes perfect sense in light of the discussion to follow.

In contrast to the nine references to Michael in the Doctrine and Covenants, Michael is mentioned only five times in all of ancient scripture: two in the New Testament and three in the Old Testament. In each case, his reference is in the context of a major conflict between the forces of good and evil. The most familiar reference, in the book of Revelation, is to Michael's battle with Satan in the premortal world:

> And there was war in heaven: Michael and his angels fought against the dragon; and the dragon fought and his angels, And prevailed not; neither was their place found any more in heaven. And the great dragon was cast out, that old serpent, called the Devil, and Satan, which deceiveth the whole world: he was cast out into the earth, and his angels were cast out with him.[11]

Then there is the strange reference to Michael in the book of Jude in the New Testament: "Yet Michael the archangel, when contending with the devil he disputed about the body of Moses, durst not bring against him a railing accusation, but said, The Lord rebuke thee."[12]

This verse appears to be quite confusing at several levels, and Bible commentators have wrestled with this passage for many years.[12] John Gill (around 1764–68) proposed that the struggle between Michael and Satan was over where—or even whether—to bury Moses' body after his death.[13] How odd for Michael and Satan to dispute over such a trivial issue. Nonetheless, this scenario—of Moses' dead body needing burial—apparently is a very old Judeo-Christian tradition. In reality, burial of Moses body was unnecessary because Moses' body was not laid in the dust, but rather, he was translated so that he had a physical body to lay hands upon and pass his keys to the Savior at the

Mount of Transfiguration.[14] An alternative explanation proposed by Gill was that the struggle between Michael and Satan occurred over Moses' spirit while he was still alive. This strange proposal, however, is completely lacking in context.

One question that may be raised concerning this quote is, where did Jude learn this story in the first place? Origen (c. 185–254), an early Christian scholar, mentioned a Jewish-Greek book, *The Assumption of Moses*, as existing in his day. The book, although considered by most scholars to be apocryphal, apparently contained a very similar account of the struggle between Michael and Satan over the body of Moses. Origen supposed that *The Assumption* was the source of Jude's account, but, unfortunately, that portion of the book is now lost.[15] There appears to be no account in extant ancient scripture of any struggle between Moses and Satan, or between Michael and Satan over Moses.

However, through modern revelation to the Prophet Joseph Smith, recorded in the Pearl of Great Price, we now have another account of "Moses' assumption," and therein is an account of Moses' struggle with Satan. We read in Moses 1:

> The words of God, which he spake unto Moses at a time when Moses was caught up [assumption] into an exceedingly high mountain, And he saw God face to face, and he talked with him, and the glory of God was upon Moses; therefore Moses could endure his presence.[16]
>
> And it came to pass that . . . Satan came tempting him, saying: Moses, son of man, worship me. And it came to pass that Moses looked upon Satan and said: Who art thou? For behold, I am a son of God, in the similitude of his Only Begotten; and where is thy glory, that I should worship thee? For behold, I could not look upon God, except his glory should come upon me, and I were transfigured before him. But I can look upon thee in the natural man. Is it not so, surely? Blessed be the name of my God, for his Spirit hath not altogether withdrawn from me, or else where is thy glory, for it is darkness unto me? And I can judge between thee and God; for God said unto me: Worship God, for him only shalt thou serve. Get thee hence, Satan; deceive me not; for God said unto me: Thou art after the similitude of mine Only Begotten. And now, when Moses had said these words, Satan cried with a loud voice, and ranted upon the earth, and commanded, saying: I am the Only Begotten, worship me. And it came to pass that Moses began to fear exceedingly; and as he began to fear, he saw the bitterness of hell. Nevertheless, calling upon God, he received strength, and he

> commanded, saying: Depart from me, Satan, for this one God only will I worship, which is the God of glory. And now Satan began to tremble, and the earth shook; and Moses received strength, and called upon God, saying: In the name of the Only Begotten, depart hence, Satan. And it came to pass that Satan cried with a loud voice, with weeping, and wailing, and gnashing of teeth; and he departed hence, even from the presence of Moses, that he beheld him not.[17]

Michael is never mentioned in this scripture, but the passage, "Nevertheless, calling upon God, he received strength," (v. 20) is very interesting. Could this be the time when Michael intervened on God's behalf to strengthen Moses and fight for Moses against Satan, as reported by Jude? Moses 1 certainly appears to contain all the requisite parameters for Jude's reference and for the missing portion of the *Assumption*. This incident also appears to be very similar to what Joseph and Oliver experienced on the banks of the Susquehanna.

The concept of being delivered by an angel is presented twice in the book of Psalms: "The angel of the Lord encampeth round about them that fear him, and delivereth them."[18] And, "For he shall give his angels charge over thee, to keep thee in all thy ways."[19] These references certainly sound like what happened to Moses in relation to Satan and Michael.

The remaining three ancient references to Michael are in the Old Testament, all in the book of Daniel, and all part of a very unusual story. According to the account in Daniel 10, Daniel had been mourning, fasting, and praying for his people for "three full weeks." Chapter 9 tells us the subject of his petition:

> Yea, all Israel have transgressed thy law, even by departing, that they might not obey thy voice; therefore the curse is poured upon us, and the oath that is written in the law of Moses the servant of God, because we have sinned against him. . . . O Lord, according to all thy righteousness, I beseech thee, let thine anger and thy fury be turned away from thy city Jerusalem, thy holy mountain: because for our sins, and for the iniquities of our fathers, Jerusalem and thy people are become a reproach to all that are about us.[20]

Then, in chapter 10, we read that beside the "great river . . . Hiddekel," "a thing was revealed unto Daniel . . . and the thing was true . . . a certain man clothed in linen, whose loins were girded with fine gold. . . . His body also was like the beryl, and his face as the appearance of lightning, and his eyes as lamps of fire, and his arms and his feet like in colour to polished brass, and the voice of his words like the voice of a multitude."[21]

Daniel said that he was the only one who saw the vision, whereas the men with him only experienced a great quaking, fled, and hid themselves. Bible commentators have identified this "man" as the angel Gabriel, who is named as the angel visiting Daniel in the previous two chapters (the only two times that Gabriel is mentioned by name in the Old Testament).

> Then said he unto me, Fear not, Daniel: for from the first day that thou didst set thine heart to understand, and to chasten thyself before thy God, thy words were heard, and I am come for thy words. But the prince of the kingdom of Persia withstood me one and twenty days: but, lo, Michael, one of the chief princes, came to help me; and I remained there with the kings of Persia. . . . But I will shew thee that which is noted in the scripture of truth: and there is none that holdeth with me in these things, but Michael your prince.[22]

This story of Daniel's prayer and answer provides us with a huge amount of information concerning the realm of postmortal spirits. Daniel was praying mightily for the release of his people, Israel, from Persian bondage, which bondage they were suffering because of their disobedience. God heard Daniel's prayer *immediately* and sent the angel Gabriel (who we learn from modern revelation was Noah in his mortal life[23]) to Persia to work for the Israelites' release. Gabriel was there fighting against the evil spirit, which controlled Persia, for *three weeks*, and ultimately had to enlist the help of Michael, the archangel, to defeat the forces of evil there.

Both Michael (Adam) and Gabriel (Noah) had already passed through their mortal probations and were now in their postmortal, eternal lives—where time apparently does not exist. Once Gabriel came back to Earth by assignment to help Daniel and the Israelites, however, Earth's temporal constraints apparently pertained to his activities. Although Gabriel struggled against the evil spirits for three weeks, he could not prevail on his own. Therefore, "Michael, one of the chief princes, came to help [him]."[22] This piece of information gives us tremendous insight into Michael's (Adam's) immense spiritual power. The mighty angel Gabriel could not defeat the evil spirits alone but had to recruit Michael to help, whose power was apparently even greater than Gabriel's. We, at present, have no more information about Michael's enormous power over evil aside from the fact that he led the hosts of heaven in the battle against Satan and his host.[11] We also do not know why other angels fall short of having such power.

In addition to Michael's great power as the defender of God's plan against the designs of Satan, whose object it is to destroy that plan, Michael (Adam) also helped create the very earth upon which this struggle takes place. In the October 1996 general conference, Elder Richard G. Scott, of the Quorum of the Twelve Apostles, stated, "Adam was Michael who helped create the earth—a glorious, superb individual. Eve was his equal—a full, powerfully contributing partner."[24]

It is very important to our understanding of our parents' nobility to appreciate what Elder Scott said about them. "Adam was . . . a glorious, superb [and we may add super-human] individual. [And] Eve was his equal."[24] Aside from Christ himself, Adam was the most powerful, spiritual being to ever live, and his wife, Eve, was his equal partner. If we want role models to emulate, these two parents of humanity are it.

Because of modern revelation, we now know that Michael (Adam) was the commanding general of the great premortal host that defeated Satan's army and cast them out of heaven. We also now know that Michael assisted the Savior in creating the earth, under God's direction. We know that Michael was designated as the "first man," Adam, the father and leader of all humanity on the earth, the Ancient of Days. We know that after Adam's life on earth ended, he returned to his role as Michael, apparently battled against Satan in Moses' behalf, assisted Gabriel in his epic twenty-one-day struggle against the evil forces in Persia, and assisted Joseph Smith in detecting Satan on the banks of the Susquehanna. We also know that, at the end of time, Michael will, once again and for the last time, lead God's forces in defeating the hosts of Satan. He will then play a major role in the Resurrection.

Adam stands at the head of the human family, not just because he is Adam, the Ancient of Days, but also because he is Michael the mighty Archangel. He, and his equally noble wife, Eve, thus stand in a place of honor and dignity throughout all eternity—the true "first family."

NOTES

1. Doctrine and Covenants 27:2
2. Doctrine and Covenants 27:3
3. Doctrine and Covenants 27:5
4. Doctrine and Covenants 29:26
5. Doctrine and Covenants 78:15–16
6. Doctrine and Covenants 88:110–111
7. Doctrine and Covenants 88:112–115
8. Doctrine and Covenants 107:53–54
9. Doctrine and Covenants 128:19–21
10. Alonzo L. Gaskill, "Doctrine and Covenants 129:8 and the Reality of Satan's Physicality," *Religious Educator*, 8:31–54, 2007.
11. Revelation 12:7–9
12. Jude 1:9
13. c.f. John Gill, *Exposition of the New Testament*, 3 vols, 1764–1768
14. c.f. *Matthew* 17:1–9
15. William John Dean, "The Assumption of Moses," biblehub.com
16. Moses 1:1–2
17. Moses 1:12–22
18. Psalm 34:7
19. Psalm 91:11
20. Daniel 9:11 and 16
21. Daniel 10:1–6
22. Daniel 10:12–13, 21
23. see *History of the Church* 3:386
24. Richard G. Scott, "The Joy of Living the Great Plan of Happiness," October 1996 general conference.

CHAPTER 4

THE INFINITE CREATION

When I was growing up and preparing to serve a mission, there were no temple preparation classes; I pretty much went to the temple cold turkey. Even though *The House of the Lord: A Study of Holy Sanctuaries, Ancient and Modern* by Elder James E. Talmage had been published in 1912 and reprinted in 1962, and *Temples of the Most High* by N. B. Lundwall had been published in 1941 and revised in 1966, I did not read either of them before attending the temple. My father died of a stroke one month before my nineteenth birthday and was not there, at least in body, to escort me through the temple. My mother and several aunts attended the endowment session when I received my own endow ment, but there were no male family members with me. I don't remember precisely what I had expected—I recall that I expected to learn some grand, eternal secrets—but I do remember being blown away by the experience. I was particularly impressed by how central the Creation story is to the endowment.

There were only thirteen functioning temples back in those days. We were in the Logan Temple District, and I had been to the Logan Temple many times to do baptisms for the dead. But my mother wanted me to go through the Salt Lake City Temple because Salt Lake was where most of her sisters lived. I was completely unprepared for the beauty and incredible craftsmanship I encountered in that temple.

In his book *The House of the Lord*, Elder James E. Talmage described the garden room of the Salt Lake City Temple as follows:

> In all its appointments it is of . . . elaborate design. Ceiling and walls are embellished with oil paintings—the former to represent clouds and sky, with sun and moon and stars; the latter showing landscape scenes of rare beauty. There are sylvan grottoes and mossy dells, lakelets and brooks, waterfalls and rivulets, trees, vines and flowers, insects, birds and beasts, in short, the earth beautiful,—as it was before the Fall. It may be called the Garden of Eden Room, for in every part and appurtenance it speaks of sweet content and blessed repose. There is no suggestion of disturbance, enmity or hostility; the beasts are at peace and the birds live in amity. In the centre of the south wall, is a platform and an altar of prayer, reached by three steps. The altar is upholstered in velvet, and on it rests the Holy Bible. On the sides of the altar are large doorways opening directly into a conservatory of living plants.[1]

As with most other experiences, words, no matter how eloquent, pale at the actual experience—especially when that experience is enhanced by the Spirit. We now have full access to several published books showing photographs of rooms in the Salt Lake City Temple, as well as those of many other temples. In addition, there used to be a beautifully accurate 1:32 scale model of the Salt Lake City Temple in the South Visitors' Center on Temple Square. Whereas those images may better prepare Saints to enter the temple than my lack of preparation fifty years ago, none of these can even come close to the actual experience.

Now, I have been back to the temple hundreds of times. My wife and I currently serve as ordinance workers in the Idaho Falls Temple, and we look forward with great anticipation each Tuesday evening to that heavenly experience. As a professional biologist and anatomist, I listen closely to the Creation story each time I attend the temple. I hang on every word spoken and deeply ponder the meaning of every word and phrase.

Elder Talmage described the temple endowment as follows:

> This course of instruction includes a recital of the most prominent events of the creative period, the condition of our first parents in the Garden of Eden, their disobedience and consequent expulsion from that blissful abode, their condition in the lone and dreary world when doomed to live by labor and sweat, the plan of redemption by which the great transgression may be atoned, the period of the great apostasy, the restoration of the Gospel with all its ancient powers and privileges,

> the absolute and indispensable condition of personal purity and devotion to the right in present life, and a strict compliance with Gospel requirements.[1]

Elder Neil L. Anderson, of the Quorum of the Twelve Apostles, in the April 2014 general conference stated, "In the temple you will learn more about the Creation of the world, about the patterns in the lives of Adam and Eve, and most importantly, about our Savior, Jesus Christ."[2]

While serving as a full-time missionary in the Great Lakes Mission, I had the privilege of reading the Book of Mormon several times. Each time I read the account of Ammon's mission to the Lamanites, I deeply pondered his teaching of King Lamoni. Ammon "began at the creation of the world, and also the creation of Adam, and told him all the things concerning the fall of man, and rehearsed and laid before him the records and the holy scriptures of the people, which had been spoken by the prophets, even down to the time that their father, Lehi, left Jerusalem."[3]

My numerous experiences in the temples of the Lord and in reading the Book of Mormon accounts have deeply ingrained in my mind the importance of the Creation story. For me personally, however, no other book can compare to the little sixty-one-page Pearl of Great Price. As a young boy growing up, that tiny, highly valued single volume lay on one of our living room end tables as a stand-alone hard-bound book with, as I recall, a dark blue binding. I recall peeking into that book and marveling at the facsimiles printed there, but I didn't read the book until I was in high school. At that time it was bound with the Book of Mormon and Doctrine and Covenants in the triple combination—and that is how I carried it into my mission field. Today, after going through numerous copies of the quadruple combination, and now carrying the scriptures with me on my smart phone, which I jokingly call my "white stone," my mission copy of the triple combination still holds a special place in my heart and resides in a special place in a drawer of my night stand. That precious missionary triple combination is color coded throughout in colored pencil, and there are copious marginal notes, as well as extra pages of notes, which I glued into the book.

Shortly after my return from the mission field in 1969, I purchased the recently published (1967) *Doctrinal Commentary on the Pearl of Great Price* by Hyrum L. Andrus. The following fall, I enrolled in a BYU course on the Pearl of Great Price taught by the author himself. That pivotal event in my life had an added bonus because a beautiful blonde coed in that class moved from the back of the classroom down to the front row, where I was seated, in an attempt to get a better grade in the course and ended up with me instead. I did have to chase her across campus in order to meet her after class. She has now been my best friend, closest companion, and eternal help meet for the past forty-nine years. There is little wonder, therefore, that the Creation story in my Pearl of Great Price is my favorite account of that great pillar of eternity.

As a prelude to the Creation story, the Prophet Joseph Smith shared this revelation in Moses 1:

> And the Lord God spake unto Moses, saying: The heavens, they are many, and they cannot be numbered unto man; but they are numbered unto me, for they are mine. And as one earth shall pass away, and the heavens thereof even so shall another come; and there is no end to my works, neither to my words. For behold, this is my work and my glory—to bring to pass the immortality and eternal life of man. And now, Moses, my son, I will speak unto thee concerning this earth upon which thou standest; and thou shalt write the things which I shall speak.[4]

We are then told in Moses 2 that:

> And it came to pass that the Lord spake unto Moses, saying: Behold, I reveal unto you concerning this heaven, and this earth; write the words which I speak. I am the Beginning and the End, the Almighty God; by mine Only Begotten I created these things; yea, in the beginning I created the heaven, and the earth upon which thou standest.[5]

Concerning the Creation of humans, we are told in Moses 2:

> And I, God, said unto mine Only Begotten, which was with me from the beginning: Let us make man in our image, after our likeness; and it was so. And I, God, said: Let them have dominion over the fishes of the sea, and over the fowl of the air, and over the cattle, and over all the earth, and over every creeping thing that creepeth upon the earth. And I, God, created man in mine own image, in the image of mine Only Begotten created I him; male and female created I them. And I, God, blessed them, and said unto them: Be fruitful, and multiply, and

> replenish the earth, and subdue it, and have dominion over the fish of the sea, and over the fowl of the air, and over every living thing that moveth upon the earth. And I, God, said unto man: Behold, I have given you every herb bearing seed, which is upon the face of all the earth, and every tree in the which shall be the fruit of a tree yielding seed; to you it shall be for meat.[6]

All of this seems quite straight-forward given our traditional understanding of the Creation. We are told in Moses 3, "Thus the heaven and the earth were finished, and all the host of them. . . . And now, behold, I say unto you, that these are the generations of the heaven and of the earth, when they were created, in the day that I, the Lord God, made the heaven and the earth."[7]

Then we seem to be thrown a curve in the third chapter of Moses. Once we have gone to all the trouble to wrap our heads around the Creation story and its implications, we are told that it hasn't actually physically occurred:

> And every plant of the field before it was in the earth, and every herb of the field before it grew. For I, the Lord God, created all things, of which I have spoken, spiritually, before they were naturally upon the face of the earth. For I, the Lord God, had not caused it to rain upon the face of the earth. And I, the Lord God, had created all the children of men; and not yet a man to till the ground; for in heaven created I them; and there was not yet flesh upon the earth, neither in the water, neither in the air; But I, the Lord God, spake, and there went up a mist from the earth, and watered the whole face of the ground.[8]

Apparently, the whole of chapter 2 is describing the spirit creation. Therefore, some of the details described there may only pertain to the spirit creation. Then follows a very strange verse: "And I, the Lord God, formed man from the dust of the ground, and breathed into his nostrils the breath of life; and man became a living soul, the first flesh upon the earth, the first man also; nevertheless, all things were before created; but spiritually were they created and made according to my word."[9]

President Brigham Young seems to have proposed that the statement "from the dust of the ground, and breathed into his nostrils the breath of life" is figurative. He stated in a talk given in the Tabernacle on October 23, 1853, "Supposing that Adam was formed actually out of clay, out of the same kind of material from which bricks are formed;

that with this matter God made the pattern of a man, and breathed into it the breath of life, and left it there, in that state of supposed perfection, he would have been an adobie to this day. He would not have known anything."[10]

Then comes the next part of the verse, which has been the source of much conflict with modern scientific data: "And man became a living soul, the first flesh upon the earth, the first man also." Is this phrase also to be taken figuratively, metaphorically, or literally as some scholars have proposed? If Adam was literally the "first flesh," then there were apparently no edible birds or mammals on the earth before Adam.[11] This concept makes absolutely no sense in the light of modern biological discoveries of fossil birds and mammals dating back millions of years. For example, the taxon Ruminantia—the ruminant mammals such as sheep, goats, cattle, deer, and antelope (the animals considered clean among the Israelites) within the order Artiodactyla— first appeared during the early to mid-Eocene, around 50 million years ago.[12]

If Adam was literally the "first man," then the scientific evidence for anatomically and functionally modern humans—over a period of 300,000 years—is negated.[13] Wouldn't it be foolish to ignore the scientifically established age of ruminant mammals and anatomically modern humans (based on thousands of data points) in the belief that four words "first flesh" and "first man" are literal rather than figurative? This is especially pertinent considering that Brigham Young suggested that the first portion of the *same* sentence *is* figurative.

Then, in the *same* sentence, we are reminded that none of this information apparently applies to the physical world anyway, for, "nevertheless, all things were before created; but spiritually were they created and made according to my word."[14] Why was this reminder inserted at the end of this particular sentence? The relationship between the spirit and physical creation is the subject matter of several chapters in my previous book, *The Infinite Creation*, and in this book. If we understand the Creation, like the Fall, to be infinite, many of the apparent conflicts between science and the scriptures allow us to increase our knowledge and understanding of this earth, its creation, and the fall.

NOTES

1. James E. Talmage, *The House of the Lord: A Study of Holy Sanctuaries, Ancient and Modern*, Produced by the Mormon Texts Project, mormontextsproject.org, Project Gutenberg, 2014.
2. Neil L. Anderson, "Spiritual Whirlwinds," April 2014 general conference.
3. Alma 18:36
4. Moses 1:37–40
5. Moses 2:1
6. Moses 2:26–29
7. Moses 3:1, 4
8. Moses 3:5–6
9. Moses 3:7
10. Brigham Young, *Journal of Discourses*, 2:6, October 23, 1853.
11. see Leviticus 7:15
12. Jessica M. Theodor, "Molecular Clock Divergence Estimates and the Fossil Record of Cetartiodactyla," *J. Paleont.*, 78:39–44, 2004.
13. Ewan Callaway, "Oldest Homo sapiens fossil claim rewrites our species' history," *Nature,* doi: 10.1038/nature.2017.22114, June 7, 2017.
14. Moses 3:7

CHAPTER 5

FINDING ALTAMIRA AND CHAUVET CAVES

Over the space of many centuries, the Fall has been rooted in the context of a vacuum. There was a perception that the Earth was very young and that Adam and Eve stepped out of the Garden of Eden into a world untouched by human hands. Science and history, however, tell a very different story.

In the early 1750s, a Scottish-born physician named James Hutton inherited his father's farm, called Slighhouses, in Berwickshire. In the process of improving his farm, Hutton observed that many of the rocks he encountered were composed of material left over from plants and animals of "ancient formation." In 1764, he and George Maxwell-Clerk made a geological tour of northern Scotland.[1]

From his travels and observations, Hutton concluded that the earth is not young and simple, but, rather very old and complex; composed, through what he called "deep time," of rocks created on the floors of ancient seas, which were then thrust up to their current locations, often high above sea level. Hutton proposed, at an 1785 meeting of the Royal Society of Edinburgh, that the modern earth was built layer upon layer over eons of years, by the same processes as seen today—a process he called uniformitarianism. This principle, the very foundation of modern geology, is that the earth has been perpetually forming, through time, by the same processes, such as erosion and sedimentation, that are occurring today. As a result of his work, Hutton became known as the "Father of Modern Geology."[2]

Charles Lyell, a Scottish lawyer and geologist, expanded upon and popularized Hutton's work in his three-volume *Principles of Geology* (1830–33). Lyell explained that the earth has been shaped by the same geological processes in antiquity as today, and that "the present is the key to the past." His conclusions, among many other findings, were based on his own research on limestone formations in Forfarshire (now Angus), Scotland.[3] The layering of the limestone led Lyell to conclude that the earth must be much older than previously thought—perhaps millions, if not billions, of years old. Subsequent research over the past nearly two hundred years has validated the uniformitarianism of Hutton and Lyell a million times over. Data obtained from numerous modern studies confirm that the earth is roughly 4.55 billion years old.[4]

Both fossil and DNA data indicate that anatomically modern humans, *Homo sapiens*, have been around for some 260,000 to 350,000 years. Most of the fossils have come from southwest Africa, but fossil remains and stone tools from *Homo sapiens* living about 300,000 years ago were discovered in 2017 at Jebel Irhoud, Morocco. These fossil remains agree very closely with DNA analysis suggesting that modern humans emerged as a separate species around 315,000 years ago.[5]

The control of fire, one of the most important technological advancements to human progress, however, predated the emergence of modern humans. Charcoal from fires in Wonderwerk Cave, Northern Cape province, South Africa, connected with *Homo erectus* occupation, have been discovered—dating from one million years ago.[6] *Home erectus* also were using spears by at least 500,000 years ago.[7]

But were those 300,000–year-old fire-making, spear-wielding *Homo sapiens* actually "us"? The renowned LDS scriptural scholar Hugh Nibley said no. In an address delivered at BYU on April 1, 1980, entitled "Before Adam," Nibley, stated:

> When science takes us to *human* prehistory, it is just more of the same. Since World War II, an immense lot of digging has been done all over the world, and the result is a great accumulation of [stage] properties but still *no play*. We learn from what is being turned up that people lived in shelters of various kinds, ate food that they gathered or hunted, warmed themselves and cooked with fire, wore clothing as they needed it, had pots to cook and store food in, had children, drank

> water, breathed air, and so on. And that is the whole story. The table is now set for the banquet, but no live guests ever show up. We sit in the darkened theater waiting for the show that never begins. It won't begin until we get a written record.[8]

Here Nibley has set his stage for the human drama, but he claims that the actors, the "live guests," apparently the "real humans," have not yet appeared. His apparent criterion for being human is the appearance of a "written record." This criterion suggests that peoples who have no written language, including people speaking several modern African languages and several Native American languages, such as Shoshone, are not fully human. He continued,

> No Adam, no play—These can't be our people. . . . Whatever is behind it, it is the culture that marks the appearance of man as such, just as by very definition it is the written record that begins his history. . . . To define true man is to discover the uniqueness of man, that which he does not share with any other creature. It can only be his culture. And when do you get a real culture? Not until you get Adam. Those 100,000–year-old villages have nothing to tell us that we do not know. It is time we got to Adam.[8]

It appears that, according to Nibley's criteria, the control of fire, which humans have not shared with other animals, is not enough to make us human; it is culture and writing that separate us. The problem is that those two criteria are quite different from each other. There is clear evidence that Neanderthals had a complex culture, including elaborate burials, but no written language. The same may be said of the Shoshone of today. Nibley concluded,

> Adam becomes Adam, a hominid becomes a man, when he starts keeping a record. What kind of record? A record of his ancestors—the family line that sets him off from all other creatures. Such records begin very early, to judge by the fabulous genealogic knowledge of the Australian aborigines (A. P. Elkin) or the most "primitive" Africans (L. Frobenius) [the supposed white "African Atlantis"?]. Even written records go back to ages lost in the mists of time—the Azilian pebbles, the marking of arrows, and the identity of individuals in their relationships with each other.[8]

A problem with the logic here is that the Australian aboriginal ancestral record was not a written record because the aborigines had no written language before the arrival of Europeans. Most of the Africans also had no written record. The Azilian pebbles, which are around 14,000 years old, have marks that may represent a primitive writing system, but they may also be purely decorative. Furthermore, the Azilian pebbles date from around 8,000 years *before* Adam.

So Nibley threw down a challenge forty years ago: find culture and you have found true humans, find someone keeping a record and you have found true humans. It appears that Nibley's criteria for "written records" is quite unclear, quite broad, and includes the oral traditions of the Australian aborigines as well as the abstract lines and dots on the Azilian pebbles 14,000 years ago. Nibley also drew a line in the sand: "No Adam, no play—These [hominids of the Olduvai Gorge and other parts of Africa] can't be our people."

Nibley didn't give a date for Adam—and, therefore, as to what precise date the line in the sand represents—but James Ussher, the Anglican Archbishop of Armagh and Primate of All Ireland (1625–56), did.[9] Ussher apparently didn't give Adam and Eve much credit for patience. He assumed that they were cast out of the Garden the very *same day* they were introduced into it—November 1, 4004 BC—only ten days after the creation of the world. According to Ussher, Adam and Eve didn't even make it twenty-four hours in paradise before eating the forbidden fruit. Even if we give Adam and Eve more credit than does Ussher, we still can set their time of expulsion from the Garden as around 4000 BC.

Given that date, it appears that the "written records" cited by Nibley, the Azilian pebbles, were decorated 8,000 years before Adam. Far more impressive than the Azilian pebbles, and first reported exactly one hundred years before Nibley's 1980 talk, was Altamira Cave, located near Santillana del Mar, Spain. The ceiling is decorated by a whole herd of now extinct steppe bison, painted around 13,000 years ago, some 7,000 years before Adam.[10] Those drawings are incredibly sophisticated. The artists who painted the bison were extremely talented and highly skilled, often diluting pigments to produce variations in hue, creating what is called a chiaroscuro effect—using strong tonal contrasts of light and dark to create the illusion of three dimensions, a technique that would not be seen again until the Renaissance some 11,500 years later. I, personally, was so impressed by those paintings that I painted a copy of one bison in oil, in 1975, and it hung on my office wall until my retirement in 2011. It now adorns one of my walls at home. There is no question in my mind that the artists who painted the steppe bison on the ceiling of Altamira Cave were cultured human beings—yet they left no written record.

Even more incredible, on December 18, 1994, three spelunkologists, Eliette Brunel-Deschamps, Christian Hillaire, and Jean-Marie Chauvet, discovered an incredible cave along the Ardèche River in Southern France, now known as Chauvet Cave.[11] That cave houses the most spectacular prehistoric art gallery ever discovered. Mostly rendered in charcoal, with some red ochre, the paintings on the cave walls, many of which had been scraped down to a light, prepared surface, depict over thirteen different species of animals in such remarkable detail that those early artists clearly had firsthand knowledge of their subject animals—most of them now long-since extinct.

For me, the most incredible, breathtaking painting in Chauvet cave is a set of four horses—the panel of horses—which are so sophisticated, so impressive in their abstract yet accurate details, including one horse, with its mouth open, clearly winded from running, that they could be cut from the cave wall and hung in the Louvre. There, they would not be considered great examples of primitive art but, rather, among the greatest works of any art ever produced.

Over eighty separate radiocarbon tests on material taken from the cave confirm the cave entrance was closed by a rock slide approximately 29,000 years ago—sealing the cave as a time capsule of ancient art.[11] This date puts Chauvet Cave 16,000 years older than Altamira Cave and 23,000 years before Adam and Eve.

Despite the great number of magnificent paintings in Chauvet Cave, there is no evidence of human habitation. Although there are thousands of bones inside the cave, mostly those of cave bears, not one single human bone has been found there. Human bones are usually found in considerable numbers in caves occupied by people. Apparently, humans never actually inhabited the cave but used it for painting and probably some now long-forgotten ceremonies—it has the feel of a primeval cathedral.[11]

No written record has ever been found for the artists in Chauvet Cave, and it is fairly certain that none will ever be found. However, throughout the cave are numerous ochre hand prints, many left by one specific artist. That artist was around six feet tall and had a unique crooked little finger (the tip of the left little finger was bent toward the ring finger). The hand prints were made by the person placing his or her hand against the cave wall and then blowing ochre through a hollow tube, such as a bird bone, leaving a negative of the hand print surrounded by red ochre. The sensitivity, the humanity, the individuality of this cave art is remarkable.[11]

In addition to being a scientist, I am also and artist and an art connoisseur. I look forward to someday personally meeting that artist with the crooked little finger and attending an exhibit featuring the collected works of the artist who created the panel of horses. Those marvelous artists who lived and painted some 30,000 years ago are most certainly "my people," and I am proud to claim them as my ancestors.

For probably hundreds of years, Turkish farmers had been clearing cut stone blocks out of their fields at Göbekli Tepe and piling them to the side. Then in 1963, the area was included as part of a routine archaeological survey by Istanbul University and the University of Chicago.[12] Klaus Schmidt of the German Archaeological Institute, intrigued by the 1963 preliminary report, went to examine the site in 1994. He recognized that the stones there were similar to some he had seen at Nevalı Çori, now submerged in the reservoir created by a dam in the Euphrates River, and began excavations at the site the following year—in collaboration with the Sanliurfa Museum—and soon unearthed the first of the huge T-shaped pillars.[13]

Since 1995, some twenty megalithic (large stone) circles, ranging in diameter from 30 to 100 feet, and containing over two hundred, twenty-foot-tall, ten-ton columns have been uncovered at Göbekli Tepe. The stone circles were comprised of six-foot-tall stone walls, and T-shaped stone columns, which may have once been roof supports. Those stone monuments, the oldest yet discovered in the world, were constructed over perhaps one thousand years around 12,000 years ago—some six thousand years before Adam. Many of the stone columns were elaborately decorated with chiseled reliefs of animals, such as bulls, boars, lions, foxes, cranes, ducks, snakes, scorpions, ants, and spiders.[14]

Göbekli Tepe is considered to have been a sanctuary of great significance in the early Neolithic period—attracting people from many miles around—right at the transition point between the hunter-gatherer era and the rise of agriculture. It is estimated that at least 500 people would have been required to cut and dress the 10– to 50–ton limestone columns from quarries, a quarter mile away, and then move them to the monument site. This megalithic monument also was apparently the site of animal sacrifice: including oxen, red deer, gazelles, boars, goats, and sheep. It is thought that this monument also may have been a center of ancestor worship.[15] Göbekli Tepe was clearly erected by a highly cultural group of people, people who remembered their ancestors—yet a people with no written language.

Dolmens are unique, single-chamber megalithic tombs, each formed by two or more large vertical stones supporting, usually one large, flat, horizontal megalithic capstone, weighing as much as 160 tons, resting on top. Whereas most dolmens were built in the early Neolithic period, about 5,000 to 6,000 years ago—around the time of Adam—some, in western Europe, were built as much as 7,000 years ago.[16] Dolmens are found all over the Old World, from Japan, China, and India in the east to Ireland in the west. They dot the map of North Africa and the eastern Mediterranean, with the highest concentration in the Middle East being the Jordon Rift Valley, and especially the Golan Heights. The greatest worldwide concentration of dolmens is in western and northern Europe: Scandinavia, Germany, France, Portugal, Spain, and especially, Great Britain and Ireland.[17] The massive dolmen stones would have required a great coordinated effort of a cultural people to move and leverage them into position.

The oldest standing stones in Europe are around 9,000 years old and located in Quinta da Queimada Menir, western Portugal.[18] There were somewhere around four thousand stone circles (henges) built in the British Isles and Brittany, between 5,300 years ago and 3,000 years ago, of which more than one thousand survive today.[19]

One of the most fascinating sites in England is the Neolithic complex at Avebury—including a standing-stone henge, over 1,000 feet in diameter (ten times as large as Stonehenge), and originally consisting of around 100 standing stones—some as much as twelve feet tall and weighing over forty tons. The Avebury henge is part of a great cultural complex including the nearly two-mile-long, stone-lined West Kennet Avenue, leading from the henge to The Sanctuary—a smaller henge with probably deep significance. The entire complex is overseen by the 130–foot-high Silbury Hill, the largest prehistoric man-made hill in Europe, and one of the largest in the world—as large as some of the pyramids of Giza, and built at about the same time. The complex was constructed over a period of several hundred years, between 4,870 and 4,220 years ago, by some great culture, which has left no written record.[20]

The presence of dolmens, standing stones, and stone circles across Eurasia, from Japan to Ireland, indicates that there were large numbers of people across those regions by five to seven thousand years ago—up to one thousand years or more before Adam. Those people were highly organized and highly motivated to build great megalithic shrines, with individual stones weighing many tons, and requiring a huge number of person-hours to construct.

A couple years ago, I was privileged to stand inside one of the most amazing and remarkable structures ever erected by human hands. One enters through a stone-encased doorway and traverses a narrow passage, barely wider than one person, sixty three feet long, terminating in a small chamber with three alcoves. We entered the chamber, about twenty people at a time, and waited for the shaft of light—in this case, furnished by artificial lights. The light illuminated the entire chamber. The hair on the back of my neck stood up from the thrill.

If you want the actual experience of sunlight rather than artificial light, during the winter solstice, you may try your luck at the lottery, along with nearly 33,000 other people from around the world each year. You may file an application at brunaboinne@opw.ie. Sixty golden tickets will be drawn each year by primary students in three local national schools: Donore, Slane, and Knockcommon. Ten lucky winners, along with one guest each, are assigned to each day: December 18–23; of course only ten of the sixty will be in the chamber on the actual solstice, December 21; the rest will see a partial lighting over the days just before and after the solstice. The sun rises over the distant horizon at 8:58 a.m., across the River Boyne, through the roof box, along the passage, to illuminate the inner chamber. Of course, you can't guarantee that it won't be cloudy—this is Ireland, after all.[21]

This magical place is called Newgrange, a 5,200-year-old passage tomb in the Boyne Valley, County Meath, a mere thirty-two miles north of Dublin. It is 600 years older than the Great Pyramid of Giza and 1,000 years older than Stonehenge. The enormous amount of time and labor required to construct this incredible monument suggests a well-organized society with a high level of culture. Yet this society had no written language.[21] Recorded history or not, the great artists and engineers of Altamira Cave, Chauvet Cave, and Newgrange are *my people, our people.* They, and the prehistoric artists and engineers of other great human creations, are children of God living in a wonderful, infinitely beautiful world.

NOTES

1. James Hutton biography, *Science Hall of Fame. National Library of Scotland.*
2. Stephn Baxter, *Ages in Chaos: James Hutton and the Discovery of Deep Time* (New York, Forge Books, 2004).
3. Roy S. Porter, "Charles Lyell and the Principles of the History of Geology," *The British Journal for the History of Science,* 32:91–103, 1976.
4. Pual S. Braterman, "How Science Figured Out the Age of Earth," *Scientific American*, October 2013.
5. C.M. Schlebusch, et al., "Southern Africa ancient genomes estimate modern human divergence to 350,000 to 260,000 years ago," *Science*, 358:652–655, 2017; see also Ewan Callaway, "Oldest Homo sapiens fossil claim rewrites our species' history," *Nature,* doi: 10.1038/nature.2017.22114, June 7, 2017.
6. Berna Francesco, et al., "Microstratigraphic evidence of in situ fire in the Acheulean strata of Wonerwerk Cave, Northern Cape province, South Africa," *Proc. Natl. Acad. Sci.*, 109:E1215–E1220, 2012.
7. Beebe Bahrami, "Finding an old flame," *The Pennsylvania Gazette*, 112:30–35, Jan/Feb 2014.
8. Hugh W. Nibley, "Before Adam," the edited text of an address given to the BYU community on April 1, 1980; publications.mi.byu.edu/fullscreen/?pub=997&index=1
9. James Ussher, *Annales veteris testamenti, a prima mundi origine deducti*, "Annals of the Old Testament, deduced from the first origins of the world," 1650; gospelpedlar.com/articles/Bible/Usher.pdf
10. José Luis López-Linares and Olivia Hetreed, *Finding Altamira*, 2016 film, directed by Hugh Hudson, Eagle Films; Samuel Goldwyn Films.
11. Much of the material in this part of the chapter was taken from *Cave of Forgotten Dreams*, History Films, Creative Differences Production; written, directed, and narrated by Werner Herzog; produced by Erik Nelson and Adrienne Ciuffo, 2010; with supplementation from other

sources, such as UNESCO/culture/World Heritage Center/The List/ World Heritage List. See also Jean-Marie Chauvet et al., *Dawn of Art: The Chauvet Cave*, English translation by Paul G. Bahn from the French edition *La Grotte Chauvet* (New York: Harry Abram, 1996).

12. Peter Benedict, *Survey Work in Southeastern Anatolia*, in Halet Çambel and Robert J. Braidwood, eds.. *Prehistoric Research in Southeastern Anatolia I* (Istanbul: Edebiyat Fakültesi Basimevi, 1980), 151–91.
13. Andrew Curry, Göbekli Tepe, "The World's First Temple?" *Smithsonian Magazine*, November 2008.
14. Sandra Scham, "The World's First Temple," *Archaeology Magazine*, 61:23, Nov–Dec 2008.
15. Ibid.
16. Vicki Cummings and Colin Richards, "How to build a dolmen," *Current Archaeology,* vol. 286, 6 December 2013; archaeology.co.uk/articles/features/how-to-build-a-dolmen.
17. map: vladimir-kovalev.blogspot.com/2013/11/zvezdnie-vrata-sri-lanki
18. Jean-Pierre Mohen, *Standing Stones: Stonehenge, Carnac and the World of Megaliths*, Thames and Hudson, 1999.
19. Aubrey Burl, *The Stone Circles of Britain, Ireland and Brittany* (New Haven, Connecticut: Yale University Press, 2000).
20. Joshua Pollard and Mark Gillings, *Avebury* (London: Bloomsbury Academic, 2004).
21. newgrange.com

CHAPTER 6

ADAM'S CREATION

We are told in Genesis 1 that "God created man in his own image."[1] However, we are informed in the book of Moses that, as with every other living thing on Earth, humans were created spiritually before we were made physically.[2] This spiritual creation was not just a planning stage, but rather the creation of spirit matter for all flesh, as we are told in the book of Numbers: "Let the Lord, the God of the spirits of all flesh."[3] The difference is that, unlike any other living thing, we were created in the express image of God[4] and in the image of His only begotten son.[5] We are told in Job that each of us has a spirit within us: "But there is a spirit in man: and the inspiration of the Almighty giveth them understanding."[6]

After we were created as spirit children of God[7] eons ago, we were created as physical beings: "The Lord God formed man of the dust of the ground, and breathed into his nostrils the breath of life; and man became a living soul."[8] Further, Adam was told by God at the time he was cast out of the Garden, "In the sweat of thy face shalt thou eat bread, till thou return unto the ground; for out of it wast thou taken: for dust thou art, and unto dust shalt thou return."[9] "Therefore the Lord God sent him forth from the garden of Eden, to till the ground from whence he was taken."[10]

Many people down through the centuries have taken these passages as meaning that God fashioned Adam like a clay doll and then literally blew into his nostrils to make him magically become a "real boy." For example, in his 1667 *Paradise Lost*, John Milton stated,

> Since higher I fall short, on him who next
> Provokes my envie, this new Favorite
> Of Heav'n, this Man of Clay, Son of despite,
> Whom us the more to spite his Maker rais'd
> From dust: spite then with spite is best repaid.[11]

Sometime in the Middle Ages, an unidentified pilgrim to "Eden" returned to England from the far eastern end of the world with a piece of clay, which "God had trimmed off as he was sculpting Adam." It's not clear how the pilgrim identified that particular piece of clay as left over from Adam's creation, but the valuable relic apparently ended up in Canterbury Cathedral, where it remained for many years and may still be there today.[12]

President Brigham Young took strong exception to the notion that Adam was made from a lump of clay. He stated in 1853:

> Supposing that Adam was formed actually out of clay, out of the same kind of material from which bricks are formed; that with this matter God made the pattern of a man, and breathed into it the breath of life, and left it there, in that state of supposed perfection, he would have been an adobie to this day. He would not have known anything. . . . You believe Adam was made of the dust of this earth. This I do not believe, though it is supposed it is so written in the Bible; but it is not, to my understanding.[13]

It turns out, now that we know much more about the chemistry and physiology of our bodies, that every human being is actually made of the dust of the earth—not as a clay doll, but bit by tiny bit. We are also all made of star dust. Stars in the early universe exploded to form gigantic clouds of dust from which solar systems, such as ours, were created. Out of the star dust (unorganized matter) within our solar system, the earth was formed. Volcanic and other violent geological activity on the newly forming earth put large amounts of carbon dioxide, formed from the earthly dust, into the atmosphere. Plants used that carbon dioxide to build tissues, along with minerals and other chemicals from the dust of the earth, absorbed through their roots. Humans eat those plants, or eat other animals that have eaten the plants, and use the molecules from the food to build our bodies. So, in a very real sense, Adam, and all other humans, are made from the dust of the earth, and after death, our physical bodies will return to the dust from whence we were taken.

Further considering Genesis 2:7, "the Lord God formed man of the dust of the ground, and breathed into his nostrils the breath of life; and man became a living soul." We recognize today that "the breath of life" is a metaphor for the spirit. For example, we can read in Ecclesiastes: "Then shall the dust return to the earth as it was: and the spirit shall return unto God who gave it."[14] People living more than a couple of hundred years ago knew that air (breath) was critical to life, but they didn't know why. The word *carotid*, the name for the main arteries to the head and brain, means "to put to sleep." Our forefathers knew that closing off the carotid arteries would induce unconsciousness and eventually death. They knew that if a person's air supply was cut off the person would die, but they had no understanding of why air (breath) was critical to survival. Many of our forefathers could write an equation: breath (air) = spirit = life. This equation would place air into the realm of some vital, mystical force, and make spirit equally mysterious, but more ethereal and common than what we now understand.

According to the 1906 *Jewish Encyclopedia*, the Jewish term *soul* means "he breathed," and is equivalent to the Latin words *anima* and *spiritus*.[15] The encyclopedia article then elaborates:

> The Mosaic account of the creation of man speaks of a spirit or breath with which he was endowed by his Creator (Gen. ii. 7); but this spirit was conceived of as inseparably connected, if not wholly identified, with the life-blood (*ib.* ix. 4; Lev. xvii. 11). Only through the contact of the Jews with Persian and Greek thought did the idea of a disembodied soul, having its own individuality, take root in Judaism and find its expression in the later Biblical books, as, for instance, in the following passages: 'The spirit of man is the candle of the Lord' (Prov. xx. 27); 'There is a spirit in man' (Job xxxii. 8); 'The spirit shall return unto God who gave it' (Eccl. xii. 7). The soul is called in Biblical literature 'ruaḥ,' 'nefesh,' and 'neshamah.' The first of these terms denotes the spirit in its primitive state; the second, in its association with the body; the third, in its activity while in the body.
>
> An explicit statement of the doctrine of the preexistence of the soul is found in the Apocrypha: "All souls are prepared before the foundation of the world" (Slavonic Book of Enoch, xxiii. 5).[15]

Yanki Tauber, writing for Chabad.com, a modern Orthodox Jewish, Hasidic website, stated,

> The soul, or *neshamah*, is the self, the "I" that inhabits the body and acts through it. Without the soul, the body is like a light bulb without electricity, a computer without the software, a space suit with no astronaut inside. With the introduction of the soul, the body acquires life, sight and hearing, thought and speech, intelligence and emotions, will and desire, personality and identity.
>
> But it is the human soul that is both the most complex and the most lofty of souls. Our sages have said: "She is called by five names: *Nefesh* (soul), *Ruach* (spirit), *Neshamah* (breath), *Chayah* (life) and *Yechidah* (singularity)."[16]

The Greek philosophers, such as Aristotle, used the word *pneuma* to mean a "vital breath," "vital spirit," "life-bearing spirit," or "soul."[17] Diogenes of Apollonia, a predecessor to Aristotle and who was quoted by Aristotle, stated, "Men and the other living creatures live by means of air, through breathing it. And this is for them both soul [that is, life principle] and intelligence . . . and if this is removed, then they die and intelligence fails."[18]

When Robley Dunglison, considered the "Father of American Physiology," wrote his book, *Human Physiology*, in 1850, there were still those who believed that blood had a life force of its own, "considered evidence that the blood may be killed; and, consequently, that it is possessed of life."[19] Dunglison recognized that oxygen is taken into the lungs and CO_2 is given off, and that respiration is in some way like combustion—that both require oxygen. Yet, he admitted, "It is manifest . . . that our knowledge regarding the precise changes effected on the air and the blood by respiration is by no means definite." Furthermore, "The cause of the development or growth of organs and of the body generally . . . is dependent upon vital laws that are unfathomable."[19]

Those unfathomable laws referred to by Dunglison are now called cellular respiration and cellular metabolism. In 1850, however, it was not even clear that cells were the basis of life, let alone what was going on inside the cell. It would be nearly one hundred years before physiologists and biochemists would discover the laws by which air, especially oxygen, relates to life. We now understand that "breath" is not life but is critical for life. We also understand that life is not a thing but, rather, is a process. Our spirits do not make us alive, but, in some way we do not as yet understand, are associated with our bodies as long as they are alive—and then at death separate from them.

The reason people die is that, for one reason or another, oxygen fails to reach the cells in sufficient amounts to maintain cellular metabolism. Carbon compounds, specifically glucose (a sugar) enters a series of enzyme-catalyzed metabolic steps called glycolysis, or the Embden–Meyerhof pathway. The Embden–Meyerhof pathway feeds into the citric acid cycle and the electron transport chain. Although many people have never heard these terms, they are foundational concepts to anyone in the fields of physiology or biochemistry. In the electron transport chain, the energy stored in hydrogen bonds (electrons) is used to produce ATP (adenosine triphosphate), the energy currency of the body—it's the ATP that keeps us alive. The last step in the electron transport chain (called oxidative phosphorylation, and worked out in the early 1940s by Herman Kalcker and others) is the transfer of an electron to oxygen. That is why the "breath," or "air," more specifically, oxygen, has to be transported through the arteries, and then the capillaries, to the tissues—where it receives the electron at the end of the electron transport chain within the mitochondria of cells. Without oxygen there to receive that electron, the electron transport chain stops completely, insufficient ATP is produced, and death follows very quickly.[20]

As will be discussed in later chapters, death was in some way suspended for Adam and Eve as long as they had access to the tree of life in the Garden of Eden. Once they were cast out of the Garden and separated from the tree of life, they became subject to death.

NOTES

1. Genesis 1:26–27
2. Moses 3:5
3. Numbers 27:16; see also Ecclesiastes 3:21
4. Genesis 1:27
5. Moses 2:26–27
6. Job32:8
7. Romans 8:16
8. Genesis 2:7
9. Genesis 3:19
10. Genesis 3:23

11. John Milton, *Paradise Lost*, book 9, lines 174–178; dartmouth.edu/~milton/reading_room/pl/book_9/text.shtml.
12. Alan Jacobs, "In Search of Eden: book review of Scafi, Alessandro, *Mapping Paradise: A History of Heaven on Earth, First Things*," Feb 2007.
13. Brigham Young, *Journal of Discourses* 2:6, October 23, 1853.
14. Ecclesiastes 12:7
15. Kaufmann Kohler, Isaac Broydé, and Ludwig Blau, *Jewish Encyclopedia*: SOUL; jewishencyclopedia.com/articles/13933–soul, 1906.
16. Yanki Tauber, chabad.org/library/article_cdo/aid/3194/jewish/What-is-a-Soul-Neshamah.
17. Abraham P. Bos and Rein Ferwerda, *Aristotle, On the Life-Bearing Spirit (De spiritu): A Discussion with Plato and his Predecessors on pneuma as the Instrumental Body of the Soul* (Leiden, Netherlands: BRILL, 2008).
18. Jason Dockstader and Diogenes of Apollonia, Internet Encyclopedia of Philosophy; iep.utm.edu/diogen-a.
19. Robley Dunglison, *Human Physiology*, vol. 2, (Philadelphia: Lea and Blanchard , 1850)
20. R.R. Seeley, T.D. Stephens, and P. Tate, *Anatomy and Physiology*, 8th edition (Dubuque, Iowa: McGraw-Hill, 2007).

CHAPTER 7

EVE'S CREATION

We first learn of Eve in the scriptures toward the end of Genesis 2: "For Adam there was not found an help meet for him. And the Lord God caused a deep sleep to fall upon Adam, and he slept: and he took one of his ribs, and closed up the flesh instead thereof; And the rib, which the Lord God had taken from man, made he a woman, and brought her unto the man. And Adam said, This is now bone of my bones, and flesh of my flesh: she shall be called Woman."[1]

In a 1976 *Ensign* article entitled "The Blessings and Responsibilities of Womanhood," President Spencer W. Kimball stated, "'And I, God, created man in mine own image, in the image of mine Only Begotten created I him; male and female created I them.' [The story of the rib, of course, is figurative.]"[2] The brackets are in the original.

Because the creation of Eve from Adam's rib is figurative and metaphorical, we can consider Eve's creation to be parallel to that of Adam, as described in the previous chapter. For example, we read in Genesis 1:26–27: "Let us make man in our image . . . in the image of God created he . . . male and female."[3]

Who is the "us" referred to in Genesis 1:26? We learn in Moses 2:26, "And I, God, said unto mine Only Begotten, which was with me from the beginning: Let us make man in our image, after our likeness; and it was so."[4] We, therefore, know that the "us" was God and Jesus Christ. However, there is more. We are told in Abraham 3:22–24:

> Now the Lord had shown unto me, Abraham, the intelligences that were organized before the world was; and among all these there

> were many of the noble and great ones; And God saw these souls that they were good, and he stood in the midst of them, and he said: These I will make my rulers; for he stood among those that were spirits, and he saw that they were good; and he said unto me: Abraham, thou art one of them; thou wast chosen before thou wast born. And there stood one among them that was like unto God, and he said unto those who were with him: We will go down, for there is space there, and we will take of these materials, and we will make an earth whereon these may dwell.[5]

Therefore, when our Savior, Jesus Christ "went down" to create the earth, including Adam and Eve, He took many of the "noble and great ones" with him. We are told in the Doctrine and Covenants 138 that those who serve in the temples, *both male and female*, were among those noble and great ones spoken of.[6] We are given even more information in Abraham 4:26: "And the Gods took counsel among themselves and said: Let us go down and form man in our image, after our likeness."[7] We can then insert the end of Genesis 1:27 to complete the picture: "In the image of God created he him; male and female created he them." These scriptures, taken together, therefore, tell us that the *Gods, male and female*, created mankind, *male and female*, in *their* likeness.

Everything that was stated in the previous chapter about Adam's creation from the dust of the earth can be restated for the creation of Eve. We now know that we are literally made from the dust of the earth, and that that dust was originally star dust. I can still see that star dust twinkling in my lovely wife's eyes. We know that violent geological activity on the newly forming earth expelled large amounts of carbon dioxide, from the earthly dust, into the atmosphere. Plants use that carbon dioxide to build their own tissues, along with minerals and other chemicals they absorb through their roots from the dust of the earth. Humans eat those plants, or eat other animals that have eaten the plants—usually after women have cooked them—and use the molecules from the food to build our bodies. So, in a very real sense, Adam and Eve, as well as all other humans, are made from the dust of the Earth.

We are told in the scriptures that Eve was given her name because she is the "mother of all living" and the "first of all women."[8] It is absurd to think of Eve as literally the mother of all living creatures—both plant and animals. But the terms are totally appropriate if considered as titles befitting her status in the infinite plan of happiness. If we consider those titles in light of infinity, even though we are not told so explicitly in the scriptures, we can be quite certain that Eve was foreordained to her noble calling, before the foundations of the earth. We also can assume that we all sustained Eve in her calling, just as we did Adam in his calling as "the first man." Therefore, in the infinite perspective, it matters not at all when Eve was actually born, she was foreordained to become "the mother of all living" and the "first of all women" in all our genealogies of the human family. We honor her in that noble position—even though generation upon generation of women had lived and died before her.

In the October 1996 general conference, President Gordon B. Hinckley stated, "Without you [women] the plan could not function. Without you the entire program would be frustrated. . . . Each of you is a daughter of God, endowed with a divine birthright. You need no defense of that position."[9]

There has been a tendency, down through the ages, to denigrate Eve as a simpleton or weakling who gave in to Satan's seductive temptation. These, however, are not the characteristics of our noble First Mother. First, modern revelation teaches that the premortal and postmortal Michael, the Archangel, was Adam in his mortal life.[10] We are also taught that Michael was the most powerful of all the angels of God—second only to Jesus Christ himself.[11] It is unfathomable to believe that the most powerful premortal spirit would choose as his future wife a spirit who was not equally powerful and noble. Second, we are told that this noble woman heard the voice of God.[12] And third, Eve was very aware of the role she played in the Fall and our subsequent exaltation: "And Eve, his wife, heard all these things and was glad, saying: Were it not for our transgression we never should have had seed, and never should have known good and evil, and the joy of our redemption, and the eternal life which God giveth unto all the obedient."[13]

Without doubt, Eve was no simpleton or shrinking violet. She stands beside Adam at the head of the human family as our great and noble matriarch. In a 1993 *Ensign* article, Elder Russell M. Nelson said of Eve: "We and all mankind are forever blessed because of Eve's great courage and wisdom. By partaking of the fruit first, she did what needed to be done. Adam was wise enough to do likewise."[14]

President Henry B. Eyring, First Counselor in the First Presidency, stated in the April 2014 general conference of the Church, "By revelation, Eve recognized the way home to God. She knew that the Atonement of Jesus Christ made eternal life possible in families. She was sure, as you can be, that as she kept her covenants with her Heavenly Father, the Redeemer and the Holy Ghost would see her and her family through whatever sorrows and disappointments would come. She knew she could trust in Them."[15]

NOTES

1. Genesis 2:20–23
2. Spencer W. Kimball, "The Blessings and Responsibilities of Womanhood," *Ensign*, March 1976.
3. Genesis 1:26–27
4. Moses 2:26
5. Abraham 3:22–24
6. Doctrine and Covenants 138:53–56
7. Abraham 4:26
8. Moses 4:26
9. Gordon B. Hinckley, "Women of the Church," October 1996 general conference.
10. Doctrine and Covenants 107:53–54
11. Doctrine and Covenants 88:112–115
12. Moses 5:4
13. Moses 5:11
14. Russell M. Nelson, "Constancy amid Change," *Ensign,* Nov. 1993, 34.
15. Henry B. Eyring, "Daughters in the Covenant," April 2014 general conference.

CHAPTER 8

ADAM AS FIRST MAN AND EVE AS FIRST WOMAN

As described in the previous chapter, the terms "mother of all living" and the "first of all women,"[1] in reference to Eve, make more sense when considered as titles rather than literal chronological statements. Indeed, we are so familiar with titles that we usually don't even think about them. For example, the president of the United States and his family are given the title "First Family." The president's wife is titled the "First Lady." It is obvious in these titles that "First" has no chronological implication. Likewise, George Washington is referred to as the "Father of Our Nation." No one is silly enough to think that George Washington is actually the biological parent of all Americans. Yet the notion that Adam was the "first man" and even the "first flesh"[2] have set many people at odds with the truths revealed through scientific investigations.

Abraham explained the right of the firstborn: "It [the high priesthood] was conferred upon me from the fathers; it came down from the fathers, from the beginning of time, yea, even from the beginning, or before the foundation of the earth, down to the present time, even the right of the firstborn, or the first man, who is Adam, or first father, through the fathers unto me."[3]

Thus, the *title* of firstborn is an infinite, eternal right that has existed since "before the foundation of the earth." That right was oftentimes, throughout history, not given to the literal first born of a certain patriarch. For example, the right of the "firstborn" was taken from Esau and given to Jacob.[4] David, who was the youngest of Jesse's sons,[5] was also made the "firstborn."[6] The Apostle Paul referred to the "church of the firstborn" as a heavenly reward: "To the general assembly and church of the firstborn, which are written in heaven, and to God the Judge of all, and to the spirits of just men made perfect."[7] Furthermore, we are told in the Doctrine and Covenants 76 that all those who enter into celestial glory are members of the Church of the Firstborn:

> That by keeping the commandments they might be washed and cleansed from all their sins, and receive the Holy Spirit by the laying on of the hands of him who is ordained and sealed unto this power; And who overcome by faith, and are sealed by the Holy Spirit of promise, which the Father sheds forth upon all those who are just and true. They are they who are the church of the Firstborn.[8]

Abraham clearly equated the "firstborn" with the "first man" in stating, "Firstborn, or the first man, who is Adam."[3] We are all, male and female, called Adam.[9] Furthermore, the right of the firstborn is given to all those, male and female, who inherit the celestial kingdom.[10]

In his first letter to the Corinthians, chapter 15, Paul compared the roles of Adam and Christ in the Great Plan of Salvation. He stated, in verses 21–23: "For since by man came death, by man came also the resurrection of the dead. For as in Adam all die, even so in Christ shall all be made alive. But every man in his own order: Christ the firstfruits; afterward they that are Christ's at his coming."[11]

Then in verses 45–47 he stated, "And so it is written, The first man Adam was made a living soul; the last Adam was made a quickening spirit. Howbeit that was not first which is spiritual, but that which is natural; and afterward that which is spiritual. The first man is of the earth, earthy: the second man is the Lord from heaven."[12]

Is the term "first man" in verses 45 and 47 to be taken literally or metaphorically? The key to answering this question may be found in verse 47, where Paul says, "The first man is of the earth." Here Paul is referring to Adam, and we don't know for sure whether "first man" is intended to be a metaphor. However, there is no doubt that the second half of the sentence, "the second man is the Lord from heaven," is intended metaphorically. Clearly, the Lord Jesus Christ was not literally the second man born on earth. This being the case, it is illogical for the first half of a couplet, "first man," to be literal and the second half, "second man," to be metaphorical. Therefore, both the terms "first man" and "second man" must be read as metaphors in this sentence. Thus, each term in this couplet should be considered more of a title than a statement of chronology. To further emphasize this point, it is clear that the term "Christ the firstfruits" is metaphorical and a title for Christ. In addition, the term "last Adam," in verse 45, is a beautiful, poetic metaphor as well.

Furthermore, in referring to Christ in his letter to the Colossians, Paul stated in chapter 1, verse 15, "Who is the image of the invisible God, the firstborn of every creature?" Here Christ, not Adam, is referred to as "the firstborn of every creature."

The implications of these metaphorical verses' literal references to the "first man" or "firstborn" are enormous. What appears to be a simple choice between these two options of a chronological "first man" or the title "first man"—a mere flip of the coin, if you will—has an enormous impact on how we understand the relationship between science and theology. If we choose the chronological "first man" option, then we create a huge gulf between science and religion, and we are forced to reject either science or religion while doggedly adhering to the other.

If we choose the option of one over the other (science versus religion), science does not come out the loser. Science is impartial; it doesn't care if it has converts. It can continue on without any believers because belief in science has no impact on the truths it reveals. Religion, on the other hand, requires faith.[13] Without faith, there is no religion. Without faith, it is impossible to please God.[14] But faith is difficult enough to practice without being forced to abandon all common sense. For example, an absolute, literal, medieval belief in the Bible story that the sun stood still upon Gibeon[15] implies that the sun rotates around the earth, whereas all the scientific data since the seventeenth century shout that the Earth revolves around the sun. Does God want us to please him by having "faith" in the archaic, medieval belief that the sun revolves around the Earth, when so believing requires us to abandon common sense? Such is not the

God I worship. My God is a God whose glory "is intelligence, or, in other words, light and truth."[16]

On the other hand, if we accept that the term "first man" is a metaphor, as the scriptures just reviewed suggest, then there is no conflict between what we read in the scriptures and what we have learned through the discoveries of science. The tipping of the scale one way or the other based on two words among the millions in the scriptures seems such a trivial issue. The gospel of Jesus Christ offers so much joy and beauty in our lives: "For God hath not given us the spirit of fear; but of power, and of love, and of a sound mind."[17] "Wherefore, fear not even unto death; for in this world your joy is not full, but in me your joy is full."[18] Those who love Jesus Christ should not fear any truth—revealed by the prophets or as revealed by science. "And as all have not faith, seek ye diligently and teach one another words of wisdom; yea, seek ye out of the best books words of wisdom; seek learning, even by study and also by faith."[19]

Should we be prepared to demonstrate our "faith" by casting aside truth as revealed by science in favor of terms in the scriptures such as "first man," which were meant to be metaphorical? The purpose of the scriptures is not to convince us that humans first appeared on Earth only 6,000 years ago. The *entire purpose of all the scriptures* is to convince us that Jesus Christ atoned for our sins and has opened the path for us to be resurrected and live our lives in such a way that we can return to the presence of our eternal Father in Heaven. That truth is not a metaphor, but it does involve a great deal of faith.

In the 1992 *Encyclopedia of Mormonism*, William E. Evenson stated, under the heading "Evolution,"

> The position of the Church on the origin of man was published by the First Presidency in 1909 and stated again by a different First Presidency in 1925: The Church of Jesus Christ of Latter-day Saints, basing its belief on divine revelation, ancient and modern, declares man to be the direct and lineal offspring of Deity. . . . Man is the child of God, formed in the divine image and endowed with divine attributes.

The scriptures tell why man was created, but they do not tell how, though the Lord has promised that He will tell that when He comes again (see D&C 101:32–33). In 1931, when there was intense discussion on the issue of organic evolution, the First Presidency of the Church, then consisting of Presidents Heber J. Grant, Anthony W. Ivins, and Charles W. Nibley, addressed all of the General Authorities of the Church on the matter and concluded,

> Upon the fundamental doctrines of the Church we are all agreed. Our mission is to bear the message of the restored gospel to the world. Leave geology, biology, archaeology, and anthropology, no one of which has to do with the salvation of the souls of mankind, to scientific research, while we magnify our calling in the realm of the Church.
>
> Upon one thing we should all be able to agree, namely, that Presidents Joseph F. Smith, John R. Winder, and Anthon H. Lund were right when they said: "Adam is the primal parent of our race" [First Presidency Minutes, Apr. 7, 1931].[20]

It may be that we honor Adam as the "primal parent of our race" in much the same way that we honor Abraham as the father of all righteous. Paul told the Galatians,

> And the scripture, foreseeing that God would justify the heathen through faith, preached before the gospel unto Abraham, saying, In thee shall all nations be blessed. So then they which be of faith are blessed with faithful Abraham. . . . For as many of you as have been baptized into Christ have put on Christ. . . . And if ye be Christ's, then are ye Abraham's seed, and heirs according to the promise.[21]

In 1839, the Prophet Joseph Smith told the Twelve Apostles and some of the Seventies,

> The Priesthood was first given to Adam; he obtained the First Presidency, and held the keys of it from generation to generation. He obtained it in the Creation, before the world was formed, as in Genesis 1:26–28. He had dominion given him over every living creature. He is Michael the Archangel, spoken of in the Scriptures. Then to Noah, who is Gabriel; he stands next in authority to Adam in the Priesthood; he was called of God to this office, and was the father of all living in his day, and to him was given the dominion. These men held keys first on earth, and then in heaven.[22]

It is clear from the Prophet Joseph Smith that Noah was "the father of all living in his day," and it is clear from Paul's statement to the Galatians that Abraham is the father of all who join the Church.

In this same light, we honor Adam as the "primal parent" of the entire human race. In light of *The Infinite Fall* it matters not one whit whether there were human beings on Earth before Adam. We honor Adam as the primal parent of the human race no matter whether members of that race were born before him or after him.

NOTES

1. Moses 4:26
2. Moses 3:7
3. Abraham 1:3
4. Genesis 26–27
5. 1 Samuel 16
6. Psalm 89:20, 27
7. Hebrews 12:23
8. Doctrine and Covenants 76:52–54, 70
9. Genesis 5:1–2
10. Doctrine and Covenants 76:52–54, 70
11. 1 Corinthians 15:21–23
12. 1 Corinthians 15:45–47
13. Hebrews 11
14. Hebrews 11:6
15. Joshua 10:12–13
16. Doctrine and Covenants 93:36
17. 2 Timothy 1:7
18. Doctrine and Covenants 101:36
19. Doctrine and Covenants 88:118
20. William E. Evenson, in *Encyclopedia of Mormonism*, eom.byu.edu/index.php/Evolution, 1992; gaps and brackets in the original.
21. Galatians 3:8–9, 27, 29
22. *History of the Church*, 3:386

CHAPTER 9

THE GARDEN OF EDEN

We are informed in the second chapter of Genesis that "the Lord God planted a garden eastward in Eden; and there he put the man whom he had formed. . . . And a river went out of Eden to water the garden; and from thence it was parted, and became into four heads. The name of the first is Pison: that is it which compasseth the whole land of Havilah, where there is gold; And the gold of that land is good: there is bdellium and the onyx stone. And the name of the second river is Gihon: the same is it that compasseth the whole land of Ethiopia. And the name of the third river is Hiddekel: that is it which goeth toward the east of Assyria. And the fourth river is Euphrates."[1]

For the majority of religious people, down through the centuries, the geographical location of those four rivers has been key to discovering the location of the original Paradise—the original Garden of Eden.

In his 2006 book, *Mapping Paradise: A History of Heaven on Earth*, Alessandro Scafi included a photograph that originally appeared in the 1944 *Times of London*.[2] The photo is of a very small white-washed brick wall about three feet tall, enclosing a space of perhaps eight or ten feet in diameter. Inside the wall is a single leaning dead tree. A hand-painted sign, balanced atop the wall and leaning against the tree states, "The Original Garden of Eden." The "garden" is in the town of Qurna, Iraq, near the confluence of the Tigris and Euphrates rivers.

If this tiny walled enclosure really was the Garden of Eden, there's little wonder Adam and Eve would have eaten the forbidden fruit and escaped as soon as possible. However, the surrounding

"Lone and Dreary World" in the photograph doesn't look all that appealing either. Alan Jacobs, in reviewing Scafi's book,[3] stated of the tree in Qurna,

> Locals call the tree the Tree of Adam, that is, the tree of knowledge of good and evil. Though living branches with leaves may be seen in the background of the photograph, my research suggests that it is not the tree of life [he seems to have confused the two trees]. It's just a tree.
>
> Perhaps not too long after that photograph was taken, the people of Qurna planted a replacement for the Tree of Adam, but it died too: It's straighter but equally bare trunk stands there today. The ironies of the scene are journalistic and irresistible, which is why the *Times* sent people there in 1944, in time of war, and again in 2003, also in time of war, to meditate upon contemporary tragedies. The problem with Paradise is that it's always Lost, of course; any meditation on it, especially in a place that claims to be its geographical location, is bound to be ironic or elegiac or both.[3]

According to the great first-century Jewish historian, Flavius Josephus,

> Moses says . . . that God planted a paradise in the east, flourishing with all sorts of trees; and that among them was the tree of life, and another of knowledge, whereby was to be known what was good and evil; and that when he brought Adam and his wife into this garden, he commanded them to take care of the plants. . . . Now the garden was watered by one river, which ran round about the whole earth, and was parted into four parts. And Phison, which denotes a multitude, running into India, makes its exit into the sea, and is by the Greeks called Ganges. Euphrates also, as well as Tigris, goes down into the Red Sea. Now the name Euphrates, or Phrath, denotes either a dispersion, or a flower: by Tigris, or Diglath, is signified what is swift, with narrowness; and Geon runs through Egypt, and denotes what arises from the east, which the Greeks call Nile.[4]

Apparently European, African, and Asian scholars, from Augustine to the Renaissance, accepted Josephus' description of the four rivers.[2] Furthermore, the concept of the Garden being "eastward" has been a bane of scholars for centuries.

Jacobs also concluded, "In reading the later chapters of Scafi's book, I found it curious that this one issue—the location of the four rivers and their correspondence, or lack of correspondence, to present-day streams—would come to dominate debate about the location of Eden almost to the exclusion of other matters."[3]

Scafi's 2006 book is a treasure-trove of ancient maps and writings concerning the location of Paradise or Eden. He observed,

> Augustine (354—430 AD) . . . argued that God had created man perfect in mind and body and that Adam had lived in a state of perfection in a physically perfect earthly paradise. . . . [A] new geographical notion of Eden was born out of Augustine's speculations on eternity and time and out of his reading of the paradise narrative as a real historical event. The question of the whereabouts of the Garden, of secondary importance for Augstine, caught the imagination of later biblical exergetes who drew out of Augustine's writings the latent geographical discourse and who named the place where map makers could put paradise. The grounds for identifying the site of the earthly paradise rested on the *Vestus Latina* (the old Latin translation of the Hebrew text of Genesis), which had explained that paradise had been planted not "from the beginning"—as Jerome rendered it in the Vulgate—but "in the east".[2]

The Northumbrian Benedictine monk Bede (673–735) was well read but not well traveled. He took the biblical term "eastward" literally and sought by study to determine where "eastward" was. Bede read Pliny the Elder's (23–79 AD) *Natural History*, where we may also read, "This our Part of the Earth of which I speak, floating, as it were, within the Occan (as hath been said), lieth out most in Length from East to West, that is, from India to the Pillars of Hercules . . . and . . . it containeth 8578 Miles."[5]

In reviewing Scafi's book, Jacobs stated concerning Bede, "The easternmost land Bede had heard of—from his reading of Pliny the Elder's Natural History—was India, so he suspected that Eden could be found there, or nearby . . . Bede [also] thought it had to be atop the highest mountain so it could escape the flood that submerged the rest of the world."[3]

Isidore, Bishop of Seville (560–636), included a discussion of the geography of Eden in his *Etymologiae* (c. 635):

> Asia includes many provinces and regions. I shall briefly list their names and locations, starting with paradise. Paradise is a place in the east, whose name translated from Greek into Latin is hortus

[garden]. Moreover, in Hebrew it is called Eden, which means in our language deliciae [delights]. The combination of the two words produces hortus deliciarum [garden of delights]. This garden is planted with every kind of tree and of fruit tree, and it also has the tree of life. There cold and heat are unknown, the air is always temperate. In the middle there is a spring watering the entire grove, which separates into four rivers. After original sin, this place was inaccessible to man; for it is surrounded on all sides by a flaming sword, that is, by a wall of fire, reaching almost to heaven. Charubim, that is, an angelic guard, is also arrayed in addition to the glowing sword to keep away evil spirits, so that the fire and the angels banish evil men and angels respectively, preventing the threshold of paradise from being crossed either by flesh or by spirit.[2]

Walafrid Strabo (808—849 AD) stated,

Some manuscripts have Eden "in the sunrise". We can conclude from this that paradise is in the east. However, wherever it is, we know that it is on earth; and that there is the ocean in between, and that there are mountains situated so as to form a barrier. [We also know] that it is very far from our world, located on high, and reaches the sphere of the moon. This is why the waters of the Flood did not touch it at all.[2]

The *Glossa Ordinaria* were annotations written in, and later printed in, the margins of biblical manuscripts, beginning in the twelfth century monastic school in Laon, France, and containing opinions of the Church Fathers. One such Glossa asserted that Paradise was an earthly garden and that Eden was a garden in the east "at an exceedingly high altitude and thus untouched by the Flood."[2]

If Eden was saved from the Flood by being atop an exceedingly high mountain, then a paradox is encountered, one that the ancient fathers seem unable to have grasped. Gardens don't do well at exceedingly high altitudes, nor do humans without oxygen tanks. Apparently, as it turns out, the most important qualification for a medieval cartographer was not to have been well traveled.

Scafi stated, "The ambiguous status of the Garden of Eden, a region existing on earth yet beyond the reach of mankind, fueled the growth of myths and legends about the earthly paradise. Endless stories were fabricated about all those heroes, adventurers and monks who attempted to reach the rainbow's end."[2]

The medieval search for the physical earthly paradise was wrapped in the same sort of mystical quest tradition as the search for the Holy Grail. There are stories of knights or monks traveling east to find Paradise, never to return. At least one paradisiacal pilgrim did return—a bishop from Gaul named Arculf. Equally amazing to the leftover clay from Adam's creation (discussed in chapter 6), Arculf found Adam's actual tomb in the Cave of the Patriarchs wherein were also buried Abraham and Sarah, Isaac and Rebecca, Jacob, and Leah—all postdiluvian patriarchs and their wives. And there is Adam, the great antediluvian patriarch. The most amazing part of this story is that the cave containing Adam's remains was preserved through the flood, was then located after Noah had apparently returned to exactly the same place from whence he had departed, was purchased by Abraham, and was used as the burial place for the later patriarchs. We know all of this from the writings of Bede, who learned about the tomb third hand.

Bede wrote, "Adamnan, priest and abbot of the monks who lived on the Isle of Iona . . . wrote a book about the Holy Places. . . . The man who dictated the information to him was Arculf, a bishop from Gaul who had visited Jerusalem to see the Holy Places."[6]

Bede wrote the words recorded by Adamnan who had written the words of Arculf, who had "actually" been there:

> In a valley one furlong to the east of . . . Hebron . . . is a double cave [the term double here apparently refers to the fact that the burials were husband and wife pairs], where the tombs of the patriarchs are enclosed in a square wall with their heads to the north. Each tomb is covered by a single stone slab, cut like those in a church: those of the three patriarchs are white, while that of Adam is of humbler and inferior workmanship, and lies not far from the others at the northern extremity of the wall.[6]

The cave is now located within the city of Hebron beneath a mosque built at the time of Saladin (1137–1193). Hebron is near Bethlehem and tours are available from Jerusalem to visit both sites, including Abraham's tomb (the Cave of the Patriarchs).[7]

It appears that eventually the enthusiasm for traveling to Paradise began to wane. Medieval travelers became more interested in the fantastic kingdom of the legendary Prester John and other such stories. The quest for the original Eden seemed to fade away.[3]

In 1442, according to Scafi, "the Venetian cartographer Giovanni Leardo" created one of the most accurate maps of the time, complete with the newest information from Marco Polo. The map was a circular representation of the world, reflecting the modern idea that the world was a [very small] sphere. The map was oriented with east at the top, as had almost all maps to that point, with Paradise uppermost. The map was divided into four quadrants by two lines, with Jerusalem located at the center where the two lines intersected. The entire Indian subcontinent was missing and Africa was divided into north and south halves, with the southern half being a great desert, "uninhabited because of heat and snakes." At the extreme eastern edge of Leardo's map, beyond Asia, at the east edge of a section labeled "India," was depicted, "an exceptionally beautiful city, with a tall column in the centre surrounded by splendid buildings, clearly labelled in red ink, and in fifteenth-century Venetian vernacular, *paradixo teresto* [earthly paradise]. . . . As it happened, Leardo was one of last to produce a map of the world showing the Garden of Eden . . . From about 1500 onwards—after the discovery of America—no map of the world showed the earthly paradise."[2]

The late medieval rediscovery of Ptolemy's maps (created about 150 AD and rediscovered around the fourteenth—fifteenth century), however, completely changed the world of map-making. Ptolemy's maps were oriented with north at the top and east to the right. As a result of Western cartographers imitating Ptolemy's map orientation, Paradise disappeared from those maps. Jacobs proposed that the maps became purely spatial geography, with all religious connotation removed—such as Jerusalem being the center of the Earth. He wondered if "what Hans Frei famously called 'the eclipse of biblical narrative' is not significantly related to the history of cartography." Furthermore, "What Weber called the 'disenchantment of the world' may have gotten a head start when mapmakers displaced Eden from its traditional place of primacy."[3]

In 1542, Bishop Augustine Steuchus, prefect of the Vatican Library, proposed that the statement in Genesis 2:8 that the Garden was planted "eastward in Eden" did not mean that it was in the far east. He argued that, rather, the Garden was "quite obviously, in Mesopotamia." He also argued that the Great Flood would have completely destroyed the Garden anyway. His contemporary, Martin Luther, agreed. Luther also agreed that the four rivers mentioned in Genesis 2:10–14, as depicted on the early maps, were wild misinterpretations of the scripture. By contrast, John Calvin apparently believed that the Great Flood had not been all that devastating and "believed that the same four rivers that flow through Mesopotamia today were the ones that flowed through that land in Edenic times."[3]

Earlier in this chapter I referred to a sign in Qurna, Iraq. There is another sign, this one in the state of Missouri, USA, which states, "Spring Hill, We are near the crest of Spring Hill which was named Adam-ondi-Ahman, Doctrine and Covenants Section 116." The heading to section 116 states, "Revelation given to Joseph Smith the Prophet, near Wight's Ferry, at a place called Spring Hill, Daviess County, Missouri, May 19, 1838." Lyman Wight had established a homestead and ferry on the Grand River at a site that became known as Wight's Ferry. The revelation itself states (the whole section is only one verse), "Spring Hill is named by the Lord Adam-ondi-Ahman, because, said he, it is the place where Adam shall come to visit his people, or the Ancient of Days shall sit, as spoken of by Daniel the prophet."[8]

In Doctrine and Covenants 107:53 we read, "Three years previous to the death of Adam, he called Seth, Enos, Cainan, Mahalaleel, Jared, Enoch, and Methuselah, who were all high priests, with the residue of his posterity who were righteous, into the valley of Adam-ondi-Ahman, and there bestowed upon them his last blessing."

The revelation recorded in section 107 was received three years before the one in section 116. It was "given through Joseph Smith the Prophet, at Kirtland, Ohio, about April 1835. . . . This section was associated with the organization of the Quorum of the Twelve in February and March 1835. The Prophet likely delivered it in the presence of those who were preparing to depart May 3, 1835, on their first quorum mission." No mention is made of Spring Hill, Missouri in this revelation. Indeed, section 116 is the only scripture to mention Spring Hill.

We are told in section 116 that "Spring Hill is named by the Lord Adam-ondi-Ahman, because, said he, it is the place where Adam [the Ancient of Days] *shall* come to visit his people" (italics added). There are two possible locations for the Adam-ondi-Ahman mentioned in

Doctrine and Covenants sections 107 and 116: 1) they are the same place, or 2) they are not the same place. Section 107 describes an event that occurred in the past, three years before Adam's death, whereas section 116 describes an event that *shall* happen in the future.

Elder Orson Pratt made the following statement in a discourse delivered in the tabernacle in Ogden, Utah, in 1873:

> Adam-ondi-ahman, the Valley of God, where Adam dwelt, was located about fifty miles north of Jackson County, in the State of Missouri. The Lord has revealed to us that Adam dwelt there towards the latter period of his probation. Whether he had lived in that region of country from the earliest period of his existence on the earth, we know not. He might have lived thousands of miles distant, in his early days. It might have been upon what we now term the great eastern hemisphere, for in those days the eastern and Western hemispheres were one, and were not divided asunder till the days of Peleg. Adam might have migrated from the great east, gathered up with the people of God in connection with the Church of Enoch, and formed a location in the western boundaries of Missouri. This is not revealed.[9]

Elder Pratt's opinion, which was common among some conservative biblical scholars, that the entire world was one body of land before the days of Peleg, is not supported by any data or any scripture, for that matter. Genesis 10:25 states, "And unto Eber were born two sons: the name of one was Peleg; for in his days was the earth divided; and his brother's name was Joktan." The earth being "divided" is never mentioned in any other scripture. Furthermore, there is no reason to believe that such division was a geological event. It is far more likely that this describes a political division. Indeed, Josephus stated, "Heber begat Joctan and Phaleg: he was called Phaleg, because he was born at the dispersion of the nations to their several countries; for Phaleg, among the Hebrews, signifies division."[10]

Jacob W. Olmstead, in his commentary on Church history, Far West, Adam-ondi-Ahman, and Doctrine and Covenants 115–17, stated,

> By revealing the location of Adam-ondi-Ahman to Joseph Smith, the Lord imbued the land in Daviess County with a spiritual history as well as a spiritual future. At a time when the development of the kingdom of God upon the earth appeared on the brink of collapse as a result of apostasy and displacement, this revelation reminded Joseph and the

> Saints of their place in an unfolding sacred history. Church leaders were now no longer solely working to establish a place for refugee Kirtland Saints and others desiring to gather, but were engaged in the gathering of the righteous to the location where Adam would one day turn over his stewardship to the Lord prior to the Second Coming.[11]
>
> Five weeks later, on June 28, 1838 with Joseph Smith acting as chair, the Adam-ondi-Ahman stake of Zion was organized with John Smith called as President.[11,12]
>
> On July 8, 1838 Joseph Smith received a revelation (now Doctrine and Covenants 117) directed to Marks and Whitney commanding them to "come forth, and not tarry." The revelation called Marks to "preside in the midst of my people in the city of Far West," presumably as the new president of the Missouri presidency. As for, Whitney, the revelation directed him to "come up to the land of Adam-ondi-Ahman, and be a bishop unto my people" (D&C 117: 10–11). Using the imagery of Adam's ancient homeland and the infinite blessings promised to Adam's posterity, the revelation queried: "Is there not room enough on the mountains of Adam-ondi-Ahman, and on the plains of Olaha Shinehah, or the land where Adam dwelt, that you should covet that which is but the drop, and neglect the more weighty matters?" (D&C 117: 3, 8) Oliver Granger, designated to settle all the Church's accounts in Kirtland, delivered a letter to Marks and Whitney containing the revelation. In the letter the First Presidency expressed confidence in the pair's willingness to obey the revelation and "act accordingly."[13] Obedient to the instruction, both Marks and Whitney forsook their possessions in Kirtland. Eventually they joined with the main body of the Saints to attend to the 'more weighty matters' of administering to the needs of Saints.[11]

Elder Bruce R. McConkie, of the Quorum of the Twelve Apostles, stated,

> Adam-ondi-Ahman, a name carried over from the pure Adamic language into English, is one for which we have not been given a revealed, literal translation. As near as we can judge—and this view comes down from the early brethren who associated with the Prophet Joseph Smith, who was the first one to use the name in this dispensation—Adam-ondi-Ahman means the place or land of God where Adam dwelt.[14]

The website Mormon Historic Sites Foundation states, "The area known as Adam-ondi-Ahman is located in Daviess County, 70 miles northeast of Independence, Missouri. It is a place of beginnings, departures and returns. This is where Adam and Eve first dwelt when they left the Garden of Eden."[15]

Several of Joseph Smith's contemporaries commented on the history of Adam-ondi-Ahman. Brigham Young stated in 1857, "Joseph the Prophet told me that the garden of Eden was in Jackson [County] Missouri."[16] Heber C. Kimball stated,

> The Prophet Joseph called upon Brother Brigham, myself and others, saying, "Brethren, come, go along with me, and I will show you something," He led us a short distance to a place where were the ruins of three altars built of stone, one above the other, and one standing a little back of the other, like unto the pulpits in the Kirtland Temple, representing the order of three grades of Priesthood; "There," said Joseph, "is the place where Adam offered up sacrifice after he was cast out of the garden." The altar stood at the highest point of the bluff. I went and examined the place several times while I remained there.[17]

In a talk given on June 27, 1863, in Provo, Utah, President Heber C. Kimball stated, "The spot chosen for the garden of Eden was Jackson County, in the State of Missouri, where Independence now stands; it was occupied in the morn of creation by Adam and his associates who came with him for the express purpose of peopling this earth."[18]

In 1994, Bruce A. Van Orden, associate professor of Church history, Brigham Young University, in response to "I Have a Question: What do we know about the location of the Garden of Eden?"[18] gave the following information:

> Relative to the locale of the site of the Garden of Eden, the Prophet Joseph Smith learned through revelation (D&C 57) that Jackson County was the location of a Zion to be and the New Jerusalem to come. The Prophet first visited Jackson County, Missouri, in the summer of 1831. The Prophet visited Jackson County again in April and May 1832. On one of the occasions, or perhaps both, the Prophet Joseph apparently instructed his close associates, and perhaps even a general Church gathering, that the ancient Garden of Eden was also located in Jackson County.[19]

According to Elder Bruce R. McConkie, President Joseph Fielding Smith has stated,

> In accord with the revelations given to the Prophet Joseph Smith, we teach that the Garden of Eden was on the American continent located where the City of Zion, or the New Jerusalem, will be built. When Adam and Eve were driven out of the Garden, they eventually dwelt at a place called Adam-ondi-Ahman, situated in what is now Daviess County, Missouri. . . . We are committed to the fact that Adam dwelt on [the] American continent.[20]

I agree with Elder McConkie, that we as a Church are committed to the concept that Adam-ondi-Ahman, in Missouri, is located very near the original site of the Garden of Eden. I personally will hold to that belief until such time as a current prophet receives revelation to the contrary. The Garden's probable isolation from the mainstream of the bulk of humanity makes the American continent an ideal location. With the flood of Noah creating a hiatus in the scriptural narrative, it is highly likely, indeed quite probable, that that flood carried Noah and his family away from Missouri, where the early biblical narrative transpires, to somewhere else on Earth such as the Middle East, where the rest of the Bible narrative picks up after the hiatus. However, as will be discussed in chapter 15, the agricultural environment into which Adam and Eve emerged after the Fall seems to be that of the Middle East, not one typical of North America.

NOTES

1. Genesis 2:8, 10–14
2. Alessandro Scafi, *Mapping Paradise: A History of Heaven on Earth* (University of Chicago Press, 2006).
3. Alan Jacobs, in "Search of Eden" (book review of Alessandro Scafi, *Mapping Paradise: A History of Heaven on Earth*), *First Things*, Feb 2007.
4. Flavius Josephus, *The Atiquities of the Jews*, in *Josephus, Complete Works*, trans by William Whiston, (Grand Rapids, Michigan: Kregel, 1960).
5. Gaius Plinius Secundus (Pliny the Elder), *Natural History*, 77–79 AD, Reprint Edition (London: Penguin Classics, 1991).
6. Bede, *Ecclesiastical History of the English People*, 731 AD (London: Penguin Books, 1990), 293–97.
7. Wikipedia: Chapel of the Ascension (Jerusalem)
8. Doctrine and Covenants 116
9. *Journal of Discourses*, Liverpool, vol. 16, 48. Discourse by Elder Orson Pratt, delivered in the Tabernacle, Ogden, Sunday Morning, May 18, 1873, reported by James Taylor, Liverpool, 1874.

10. Flavius Josephus, *The Atiquities of the Jews*, in *Josephus, Complete Works*, trans by William Whiston, Kregel (Grand Rapids, MI, 1960), Book I, Chapter VI, paragraph 4.
11. LDS.org: Church History Far West and Adam-ondi-Ahman, D&C 115, 116, 117, Jacob W. Olmstead, September 12, 2013.
12. Conference Minutes, *Elders' Journal* 1 no., August 4, 1838, 60–61.
13. Joseph Smith, Sidney Rigdon, and Hyrum Smith to William Marks and Newel K. Whitney, July 8, 1838, josephsmithpapers.org, August 19, 2013.
14. Bruce R. McConkie, *Mormon Doctrine* (Salt Lake City: Deseret Book, 1958), 19–20.
15. Mormon Historic Sites Foundation; mormonhistoricsites.org
16. Journal of Wilford Woodruff, vol. 5, Mar. 15, 1857, Archives Division, Church Historical Dept., Salt Lake City; as cited by Bruce A. Van Orden, "I Have a Question: What do we know about the location of the Garden of Eden?," *Ensign*, January, 1994; also see LDS.org: garden of eden location.
17. Orson F. Whitney, *Life of Heber C. Kimball* (1st Edition—1888, Unabridged with an Index): *An Apostle, The Father and Founder of the British Mission* (Classic LDS Biography Series, Volume 1), (CreateSpace Independent Publishing Platform, 2017), 209–210.
18. *Journal of Discourses*, vol. 10, 235, Discourse by President Heber C. Kimball, delivered in Provo City, June 27, 1863. Reported by J. V. Long, Liverpool, 1865.
19. Bruce A. Van Orden, "I Have a Question: What do we know about the location of the Garden of Eden?," *Ensign* January, 1994; also see LDS. org: garden of eden location.
20. Bruce R. McConkie, *Doctrines of Salvation*, 3:74 (Salt Lake City: Bookcraft, 1956).

CHAPTER 10

ADAM AND EVE BEFORE THE GARDEN

We read in the book of Genesis that Adam was the first to be introduced into the Garden of Eden: "And the Lord God took the man, and put him into the garden of Eden to dress it and to keep it."[1] Next, after commanding Adam not to partake "of the tree of the knowledge of good and evil,"[2] God mentioned that Adam needed a companion: "And the Lord God said, It is not good that the man should be alone; I will make him an help meet for him."[3] But before a companion was found for Adam, according to the account, "God formed every beast of the field, and every fowl of the air; and brought them unto Adam to see what he would call them: and whatsoever Adam called every living creature, that was the name thereof."[4]

This part of the Genesis story seems to me to be an apocryphal tale. First of all, there are over ten thousand living species of "fowl of the air" alone,[5] and their geographical restrictions would have been problematic for lining them up to count. For example, the vast majority of the 338 known species of hummingbirds are found only in the subtropical forests of the northern Andes of South America.[6] Three hundred sixty species of birds are found only in Australia.[7]

Furthermore, if Adam named "every living creature," then he would have spent many months coming up with enough names for the 360,000 species of beetles (Coleoptera), which account for 25 percent of all "living creatures."[8] As J.B.S. Haldane is credited with saying: God apparently has "an inordinate fondness for beetles."[9] The line for beetles alone must have been several miles long.

Fortunately for Adam, 99 percent of the estimated five billion species that have ever lived on the earth were already extinct.[10] But that still left around 8.7 million total species of plants and animals living at his time, of which roughly 80 percent were animals. He also apparently either didn't complete the job or most of the names he gave the animals have since been lost, because an estimated 86 percent of all living creatures on Earth and 91 percent of species in the ocean have not yet been described.[11] Furthermore, it is not clear if all the living creatures included the fishes and other aquatic animals. If so their lining up to be named would have posed another major problem.

In 2003 and again in 2004, 102 researchers over 24,354 person-days, surveyed arthropod (spiders and insects) species in a 0.48 hectare area of the San Lorenzo Protected Area in Panama. They identified 129,494 arthropods in 6144 focal species (species that define the sensitivity and uniqueness of a given habitat type) within that area of tropical rain forest. From this survey, they estimated that a single hectare of rain forest is inhabited by some 18,439 species.[12]

The accounts of Adam naming the animals in Moses 3:19–20 and Abraham 5:20–21 both retain the phrase "every living creature," even though Moses 3:19 is expanded by the addition of extra phrases compared to the Genesis account and the term "the Lord God" in Genesis 2:19 is changed to "the Gods" in Abraham 5:20. If the story in Genesis is apocryphal, that same apocryphal part was retained in the Moses and Abraham accounts. I am not aware that any Church leader or other authority has ever commented on this issue except to refer to the story as written. Suggesting that the story of Adam naming the animals is an apocryphal tale that at some point was inserted into the scriptures and was retained in modern versions of those scriptures, in my opinion, in no way diminishes the validity of the rest of the story of Adam and Eve.

It is interesting that in the Abrahamic account of the Creation, Eve is created before every living creature is brought to Adam to name.[13]

Concerning Eve's creation, we are told in all three accounts that God took one of Adam's ribs and made a woman.[14] President Spencer

W. Kimball has said, "The story of the rib, of course, is figurative."[15] With the rib story being "figurative," what is the "real" story? Were Adam and Eve magically created in the Garden of Eden, or did they have some previous existence? At least for Adam, we are told he was made somewhere else before he was "put . . . into the garden of Eden."[16]

One of the timeless questions with which Adam and Eve's children have wrestled for centuries is, did Adam and Eve have navels (umbilicus, belly buttons)? The great *Renaissance* painters all seemed to believe that Adam and Eve needed to be depicted with them. For example, navels were included for both Adam and Eve in Albrecht Dürer's *Adam and Eve* (1507), Michelangelo's *The Fall of Adam and Eve*, (Sistine Chapel, c. 1510), Lucas Cranach the Elder's *Eve Giving Adam the Forbidden Fruit* (1526), Titian's *Adam and Eve* (1550), and Peter Paul Rubens' *Adam and Eve* (c. 1600). In Michelangelo's famous Sistine Chapel fresco, *The Creation of Adam* (c. 1512), not only did Michelangelo depict Adam with a navel, but God also has a navel beneath His robes!

Apparently, although the *Renaissance* artists included navels in their paintings, the early Catholic Church philosophers never addressed the issue.[17] Then, in the middle of the nineteenth century, an English naturalist, inventor of the saltwater aquarium, and minister of the Plymouth Brethren, Philip Henry Gosse took on the issue—with gusto. In his 1857 book, *Omphalos: An Attempt to Untie the Geological Knot* (*omphalos* is Greek for navel),[18] Gosse proposed that Adam, who had no mother and was created as a fully grown man, had a navel because God wanted to give him the *appearance* of having human ancestry. Gosse also reasoned that the fossil record had been created by God to give the *allusion* of antiquity. Gosse was well aware of Charles Darwin and had even attended some of his lectures. He was also familiar with the writings of Charles Lyell on geological stratification, and Gosse was anxious to reconcile Lyell's work with the biblical creation.

Gosse hoped the *Omphalos* would be widely read and that it would explain science in light of what he perceived as the biblical creation story. It did neither. The principal review of *Omphalos* was written by Gosse's poet son, Edmund Gosse, in his book *Father and Son* in 1907:

> Never was a book cast upon the waters with greater anticipation of success than was this curious, this obstinate, this fanatical volume. . . .

> He offered it with a glowing gesture to atheists and Christians alike. This was to be a universal panacea; this the system of intellectual therapeutics which could not but heal all the maladies of the age. But alas, atheists and Christians alike looked at it and laughed, and threw it away.[19]

Gosse portrayed his father as an unremitting, uncompromising despot of religious dogmatism. In an earlier, 1896 review of his father's book, Edmund Gosse wrote,

> Life is a circle, no one stage of which more than any other affords a natural commencing-point. Every living object has an omphalos, or an egg, or a seed, which points irresistibly to the existence of a previous living object of the same kind. Creation, therefore, must mean the sudden bursting into the circle, and its phenomena, produced full grown by the arbitrary will of God, would certainly present the stigmata of a pre-existent existence. Each created tree would display the marks of sloughed bark and fallen leaves, though it had never borne those leaves or that bark. The teeth of each brute would be worn away with exercise which it had never taken. By innumerable examples he shows that this must have been the case with all living forms. If so, then why may not the fossils themselves be part of this breaking into the circle? Why may not the strata, with their buried fauna and flora, belong to the general scheme of the prochronic development of the plan of the life-history of this globe?[20]

Henry Gosse asked the Reverend Charles Kingsley, an Anglican priest, university professor, historian, novelist, and author of children's novel *The Water Babies, A Fairy Tale for a Land Baby*, to write a review of *Omphalos*. Kingsley was a friend of Gosse, but he was also a friend of Charles Darwin. Kingsley refused to write a review for *Omphalos*, but he wrote a letter to Gosse:

> Shall I tell you the truth? It is best. Your book is the first that ever made me doubt, and I fear it will make hundreds do so. Your book tends to prove this—that if we accept the fact of absolute creation, God becomes *Deus quidam deceptor* [God who is sometimes a deceiver]. I do not mean merely in the case of fossils which *pretend* to be the bones of dead animals; but in the one single case of your newly created scars on the pandanus trunk, your newly created Adam's navel, you make God tell a lie. It is not my reason, but my *conscience* which revolts here... I cannot... believe that God has written on the rocks one enormous and superfluous lie for all mankind.[21]

Apparently no other reviews of *Omphalos* were ever written except by Edmund. Then, in 1987, Stephen Jay Gould used reference to Gosse's *Omphalos* as a launching platform for his essay, "Adam's Navel."[4] Gould stated,

> But what is so desperately wrong about *Omphalos*? Only this really (and perhaps paradoxically): that we can devise no way to find out whether it is wrong—or for that matter, right. *Omphalos* is the classical example of an utterly untestable notion, for the world will look exactly the same in all its intricate detail whether fossils and strata are prochronic or products of an extended history.[22]

Gould said, "I am not, personally, a believer or a religious man in any sense of institutional commitment or practice. But I have a great respect for religion, and the subject has always fascinated me, beyond almost all others (with a few exceptions, like evolution and paleontology)."[23]

He also stated, "The most erroneous stories are those we think we know best—and therefore never scrutinize or question."[24]

Science is testable; that's its strength. Religion, on the other hand, as faith based, is largely untestable. That is not to say we can't conduct "experiments" in faith.[25] Nonetheless, as real as they are, the "results" of faith experiments are founded on feelings,

> Now, we will compare the word unto a seed. Now, if ye give place, that a seed may be planted in your heart, behold, if it be a true seed, or a good seed, if ye do not cast it out by your unbelief, that ye will resist the Spirit of the Lord, behold, it will begin to swell within your breasts; and when you feel these swelling motions, ye will begin to say within yourselves—It must needs be that this is a good seed, or that the word is good, for it beginneth to enlarge my soul; yea, it beginneth to enlighten my understanding, yea, it beginneth to be delicious to me.[26]

"Enlargement of the soul" can't be measured by any current scientific method and, therefore, is not admissible as a published, scientific study. This, *The Infinite Fall*, is largely based on faith. It is not my intent, as it was Gosse's, to shoehorn scientific data into a preconceived notion of what is perceived to be "religion," but much of which is philosophy, mingled with scanty scripture—and in many cases, mingled with no scripture at all. It is also not my intent in this book to model true religion into the image of science. On the contrary, my objective is to merely point out that many beliefs we label as "religion" have no basis in scripture, and are metaphor, allegory, or, oftentimes, simply tradition.

So what can we conclude about Adam and Eve's navel—and thus their origins? In a talk given in the Salt Lake Tabernacle on October 9, 1859, President Brigham Young stated,

> Here let me state to all philosophers of every class upon the earth, when you tell me that Father Adam was made as we make adobes from the earth, you tell me what I deem an idle tale. When you tell me that the beasts of the field were produced in that manner, you are speaking idle words devoid of meaning. There is no such thing in all the eternities where the Gods dwell. Mankind are here because they are the offspring of parents who were first brought here from another planet, and power was given them to propagate their species, and they were commanded to multiply and replenish the earth.[27]

I certainly respect President Young in his calling as the second prophet of the Church, and I admire him for his intellect and willingness to think outside the box. I fully agree with President Young's conclusion that we are the "offspring of parents." However, there were many times in his discourses from the pulpit that he gave his own opinions,[28] and I certainly believe that humans coming from another planet was one of those times.

Overwhelming data from the modern field of genetics, of which President Young knew nothing, precludes humans coming from anywhere different from the rest of the animal world on the Earth. If humans came here from another planet, then all other animals came here from the *same* planet. Our DNA is not alien when compared to the DNA of other animals—we are kindred beings. We are spirit children of our Heavenly Father, but our bodies were created from the dust of *this* earth.

Had Brigham Young been aware of the scientific data of today, I am confident he would agree with it—reversing his opinion that humans came from another planet. He was not an opponent of science—quite the contrary. In May 1874, he stated:

> The idea that the religion of Christ is one thing, and science is another, is a mistaken idea, for there is no true religion without true

> science, and consequently there is no true science without true religion. The fountain of knowledge dwells with God, and he dispenses it to his children as he pleases, and as they are prepared to receive it, consequently it swallows up and circumscribes all.[29]

I firmly believe that in 1859, members of the Church were not prepared to receive the full story concerning the earthly origins of Adam and Eve's physical bodies. President Young's 1874 statement suggests to me that one way God dispenses knowledge to His children is through scientific discovery, and I believe that today we are nearly ready to receive that new information.

During the April 2003 general conference of the Church, President Gordon B. Hinckley stated,

> Every man or woman who ever walked the earth, even the Lord Jesus, was once a boy or girl like you. They grew according to the pattern they followed. If that pattern was good, then they became good men and women.
>
> Never forget, my dear young friends, that you really are a child of God who has inherited something of His divine nature.[30]

Apparently the statement, "Every man or woman who ever walked the earth . . . was once a boy or girl like you," also includes Adam and Eve.

In 1909, the First Presidency of the Church, under the presidency of President Joseph F. Smith, made the following statement:

> True it is that the body of man enters upon its career as a tiny germ embryo, which becomes an infant, quickened at a certain stage by the spirit whose tabernacle it is, and the child, after being born, develops into a man. There is nothing in this, however, to indicate that the original man, the first of our race, began life as anything less than a man, or less than the human germ or embryo that becomes a man.[31]

Therefore, we may conclude from the above statements, and from the overwhelming scientific evidence, that somewhere, on Earth, Adam and Eve began life like every other human being that has ever lived, first as human embryos and then as a boy and girl who, when sufficiently mature, were placed by God into the Garden of Eden and, apparently, their memories of previous Earthly connections were erased—not a difficult task, which we now call amnesia.

Adam and Eve were selected from before the foundations of the world to represent the entire human family in the Fall, which was an integral part of the eternal plan of happiness. We all—every human being—every *Homo sapiens*—that has ever lived, whether 200,000 years ago or born yesterday, agreed to Adam and Eve's representing us in the Fall. The *infinite* nature of the Fall made time, and thus chronology, completely irrelevant. Adam and Eve both had lives before the Garden of Eden, but those lives have not as yet been revealed to us. They are to us the "first man" and "first woman" with whom we are to deal scripturally.

NOTES

1. Genesis 2:15
2. Genesis 2:16–17
3. Genesis 2:18
4. Genesis 2:19
5. Tim Birkhead, Jo Wimpenny, Jo, and Bob Montgomerie, *Ten Thousand Birds: Ornithology since Darwin* (Princeton, NJ: Princeton University Press, 2014).
6. J. Fjeldså and I. Heynen, *Genus Oreotrochilus*, 623–24, in: J. del Hoyo, A. Elliott, and J. Sargatal, eds. *Handbook of the Birds of the World*, vol. 5, *Barn-owls to Hummingbirds* (Barcelona: Lynx Editions, 1999).
7. Louise Egerton, ed. *Encyclopedia of Australian wildlife* (Sydney: Reader's Digest, 2005).
8. P. Bouchard, V.V. Grebennikov, A.B.T. Smith, and H. Douglas, *Biodiversity of Coleoptera*, 265–301. In R.G. Foottit and P.H. Adler, eds. *Insect biodiversity: science and society* (Oxford: Blackwell Publishing, 2009).
9. Stephn J. Gould, "A Special Fondness for Beetles," *Natural History*, January 1993.
10. Mark Newman, "A model of mass extinction," *Journal of Theoretical Biology,* 189:235–252, 1997.
11. Camilo Mora, Derek P. Tittensor, Sina Adl, Sina, Alastair G. Simpson, and Boris Worm, "How Many Species Are There on Earth and in the Ocean?" *PLoS Biol.*, journals.plos.org/plosbiology/article?id=10.1371/journal.pbio.1001127, 2011.
12. Yves Basset, et al., "Arthropod Diversity in a Tropical Forest," *Science* 338:1481–1484, 2012.
13. Abraham 5:14–21
14. Genesis 2:21–22
15. Spencer W. Kimball, "The Blessings and Responsibilities of Womanhood,"

Ensign, March 1976.

16. Genesis 2:15
17. whynotcatholicism.net/view/adam-and-eve-and-science
18. Philip Henry Gosse, *Omphalos: An Attempt to Untie the Geological Knot*, van Voorst, London, 1857, gutenberg.org/ebooks/39910.
19. Edmund Gosse, *Father and Son* (Portsmouth, NH: Heinemann, 1907).
20. Edmund Gosse, *The naturalist of the sea-shore; the life of Philip Henry Gosse* (London: William Heineman, 1896), 278.
21. Garrett Hardin, *Naked Emperors: Essays of a Taboo-Stalker*, William Kaufmann, 1982.
22. Stephen J. Gould, *The Flamingo's Smile* (Penguin Books, 1987); see also Gould, *Adam's Navel* (Penguin Books, 1995).
23. Stephen J. Gould, *Leonardo's Mountain of Clams and the Diet of Worms: Essays on Natural History* (Three Rivers Press), 1998, 281.
24. Stephen J. Gould, *Full House: The Spread of Excellence from Plato to Darwin* (Three Rivers Press, 1997), 57.
25. c.f. Alma 32
26. Alma 32:28
27. Brigham Young, as recorded by G.D. Watt, *Journal of Discourses*, 7:285, 1859.
28. c.f. *Journal of Discourses*, 1:339; 7:331; 14:42
29. Brigham Young, as reported by David W. Evans, *Journal of Discourses*, 17:52, May 3, 1874.
30. Gordon B. Hinckley, "You Are a Child of God," April 2003 general conference.
31. Joseph F. Smith, John R. Winder, and Anthon H. Lund, "God created man in his own image," *Improvement Era,* Nov. 1909, 75–81; reprinted in the Feb. 2002 *Ensign*, lds.org/ensign/2002/02/the-origin-of-man?lang=eng.

CHAPTER 11

CONDITIONS IN THE GARDEN

We are told about conditions in the Garden of Eden very briefly in the books of Genesis and Moses. Genesis 2 says: "And the Lord God planted a garden eastward in Eden. . . . And out of the ground made the Lord God to grow every tree that is pleasant to the sight, and good for food; the tree of life also in the midst of the garden, and the tree of knowledge of good and evil."[1]

These verses in Genesis tell us that the Garden was full of trees and that man [Adam] was apparently initially alone. Moses 3:9 provides more details about the trees:

> And out of the ground made I, the Lord God, to grow every tree, naturally, that is pleasant to the sight of man; and man could behold it. And it became also a living soul. For it was spiritual in the day that I created it; for it remaineth in the sphere in which I, God, created it, yea, even all things which I prepared for the use of man; and man saw that it was good for food. And I, the Lord God, planted the tree of life also in the midst of the garden, and also the tree of knowledge of good and evil.[2]

Here we are told that every tree in the Garden was a living soul—spiritual—and "remaineth in the sphere in which I, God, created it." We are also told that the trees grew "naturally," that is, apparently, from the seeds of other trees, which had dropped into the rich earth of the

Garden. That rich earth would have been created by numerous plants dying and decaying over many years to create the rich, dark compost of the Garden. Dark soil is organic soil, and organic soil is made from dead and decaying plants. Soil that is not enriched by organic matter is unfit for gardening.

We are also told that the trees were good for food. Although fruit is not mentioned in those verses, we are told in Genesis 1:11 that the fruit trees were yielding fruit, "whose seed is in itself." Therefore, it appears that, in the Garden of Eden, man [Adam] was eating fruit, and perhaps even nuts, from the trees growing naturally there. In order for Adam to eat fruit from the trees in the Garden, at least two criteria must be met: first, the trees must be reproducing, which is the process by which fruit is formed. Second, the fruit must die in the process of being eaten. Not a single scripture states that the trees were in any way immortal or infertile.

Although we are told in Genesis 1:29 that man and woman were given "every herb bearing seed" for food, it was not until Genesis 3:18, as Adam and Eve were being cast out of the Garden, that they were told they would be eating herbs. It is possible, therefore, that they were eating only fruit, and maybe nuts, in the Garden. Of course, reference to "eating herbs" may have been metaphorical—referring to a harsher life than they had enjoyed in the Garden. Adam was told specifically that, with one exception, he could eat "of every tree of the Garden."[3] It also appears that the man [Adam] was working in the Garden—dressing it and keeping it.[4]

As to animals in the Garden, we are given no information other than "every beast of the field, and every fowl of the air" were brought to Adam "to see what he would call them."[5] We are not told whether there were animals residing in the Garden, besides those merely brought in to be named.

Only after Adam named the animals[6] is the creation of Eve from Adam's rib described.[7] We know that the story of the rib is figurative.[8] The concept of a rib, however, is very interesting and may provide insight into conditions within the Garden. "And Adam said, This is now bone of my bones, and flesh of my flesh: she shall be called Woman, because she was taken out of Man."[9] First of all, if this entire story is figurative, then Adam may not have uttered those immortal words. If he did say what is claimed, how did he know about bones without having seen bones of dead animals? God may have taught Adam about bones, but that would have been like teaching an anatomy course without a lab, which is not very effective. The concept of flesh and bone must be learned by experience, without which the terms are meaningless. Whereas the vast majority of Adam's experiences were to come after he was expelled from the Garden, if he actually referred to flesh and bone while still in the Garden, he must have had *some* experiences therein.

Two trees are specifically mentioned in the Garden, "the tree of life also in the midst of the garden, and the tree of knowledge of good and evil."[10] We are not told that Adam was given any specific instructions concerning the tree of life. We are only told, "And the Lord God commanded the man, saying, Of every tree of the garden thou mayest freely eat: But of the tree of the knowledge of good and evil, thou shalt not eat of it, nevertheless, thou mayest choose for thyself, for it is given unto thee; but, remember that I forbid it, for in the day thou eatest thereof thou shalt surely die."[11]

Two points are of interest here. First, Adam apparently was given this command before Eve was even on the scene in the Garden, so Eve must have been taught this commandment at some later, unspecified time. Second, Adam was told that if he ate of the tree of knowledge of good and evil he would "surely die." How would Adam even know what to die meant if he had never seen death? This warning strongly suggests that Adam had already had experience with seeing death of something, apparently of animals with bones, and not just that of fruit.

We are not told the function of the tree of life until after Adam and Eve were cast out of the Garden.[12] This function will be discussed in later chapters. Also we are not told whether, before the Fall, Adam was told what the tree of life did, or whether it was any different from any other tree in the Garden. However, we are told in 2 Nephi that "if Adam had not transgressed he would not have fallen, but he would have remained in the garden of Eden. And all things which were created must have remained in the same state in which they were after they were created; and they must have remained forever, and had no end."[13]

Some people have interpreted this scripture to mean that there was no death of *anything* before the Fall. However, that is not what this scripture is teaching. The key phrase here is "and they must have remained forever, and had no end." The word "they" in this phrase is a pronoun, and as such, must modify the nearest previous noun, which, in this case is "things." Therefore, grammatically, "things" may replace "they" in the phrase "and things must have remained forever, and had no end." We can even add the adjective "all" to the phrase: "and all things must have remained forever, and had no end." That certainly sounds like there was no death of *anything* before the Fall. But let's read the next verse: "And they would have had no children; wherefore they would have remained in a state of innocence, having no joy, for they knew no misery; doing no good, for they knew no sin."[14]

Replacing "things" for "they" we get, "And things would have had no children; wherefore things would have remained in a state of innocence, having no joy, for things knew no misery; doing no good, for things knew no sin." If we replaced the words "things" or "they" with a noun for any other living thing except humans, say for example zebra, verse 23 becomes nonsensical: "And zebras would have had no children; wherefore zebras would have remained in a state of innocence, having no joy, for zebras knew no misery; doing no good, for zebras knew no sin." We do not use the term "children" when we refer to the offspring of zebras. We also do not think of zebras capable of sinning. It is clear from this verse that the "things" and "they" referred to in verse 22 did not mean zebras, or any other non-human living thing; they were specifically Adam and Eve. We still use the same type of language today: "If I had left ten minutes earlier, things would have turned out differently."

Many people have grown up believing that there was no death of *anything* before the Fall. There is *not one single scripture* anywhere that teaches any such thing. Such beliefs have come from the philosophies of men. We may begin with a statement by Pope Gregory I (c. 540–604) in a letter (c. 600 AD) to Augustine of Canterbury (early 6th century–604): "For when our first parents sinned in the Garden, they justly forfeited God's gift of immortality."[15] Then comes the classic statement by the great English scholar and poet John Milton (1608–1674), who put the following words into God's mouth: "I, at first, with two fair gifts Created him endowed; with happiness, And immortality: that fondly lost."[16]

Thanks to the insinuated philosophies of these and other great and influential thinkers, the vast majority of religious people, even today, believe that the entire earth was a paradise before the Fall and there was no death of anything. This view, however, is held in the face of *not one single supporting scripture*. It is time we put off the philosophies of men, in this case, not even mingled with scripture, and ponder the actual scriptures more carefully.

In addition to the scriptures, we now know far more about human anatomy and physiology than was known in the seventeenth century, or even the nineteenth century. If there was no death of *anything* before the Fall, Adam and Eve, as well as the garden itself, would look quite different from anything we can imagine. In addition to a rich garden requiring dead plants for compost, without cell death, none of the trees in the garden would have had bark. Without cell death, Adam and Eve would have had no hair, no fingernails, and no skin. In short, they wouldn't have been a very pretty sight. It is my opinion that most people's notion of immortality and life in the Garden of Eden is quite wide of the mark.

I believe in a literal Adam and Eve. I believe in a literal Garden of Eden. I believe in a literal tree of life. But I believe that the imaginations of our ancestors have greatly clouded the picture of the actual conditions in the Garden. I also believe that some parts of the story surrounding the Garden of Eden are just that—a story—like the story about God bringing all the animals to Adam so he could name them. Whether or not Adam named the animals is not critical to our faith in his infinite, eternal role in our progression. However, putting off the fantasies concerning the Garden of Eden built up over the centuries by the well-meaning philosophies of men is critical to our correct understanding of *The Infinite Fall*. President Russell M. Nelson (while serving as an apostle) stated,

> In a very real way, the atonement of Jesus Christ affects each of our lives and the life of every human being who ever lived. Understanding the significance of His atonement is fundamental to choices we make in all facets of our lives. The atonement of the Lord is central to our faith.
>
> We are scripturally bound to study it and to teach it. . . .
>
> But before one can comprehend the *atonement* of Christ, one must first understand the *fall* of Adam. And before one can comprehend the fall of Adam, one must first understand the *Creation*. These three pillars of eternity relate to one another.[17]

NOTES

1. Genesis 2:8–9
2. Moses 3:9
3. Genesis 2:16
4. Genesis 2:15
5. Genesis 2:19
6. Genesis 2:20
7. Genesis 2:21–22
8. Spencer W. Kimball, "The Blessings and Responsibilities of Womanhood," *Ensign*, March 1976, *lds.org/ensign/1976/03/the-blessings-and-responsibilities-of-womanhood?lang=eng.*
9. Genesis 2:23
10. Genesis 2:9
11. Genesis 2:16–17
12. Genesis 3:22–24; see also Alma 12:21–23
13. 2 Nephi 2:22
14. 2 Nephi 2:23
15. Bede, *Ecclesiastical History of the English People*, 731 AD; translated by Leo Sherley-Price (Penguin, 1955, 1990), 82–84.
16. John Milton, *Paradise Lost*, Book XI, *The Argument*, 1667.
17. Russell M. Nelson, "Standards of the Lord's Standard-Bearers," *Ensign,* Aug. 1991, 5–6; italics in original.

CHAPTER 12

CONDITIONS OUTSIDE THE GARDEN

The scriptures tell us nothing about conditions outside the Garden of Eden. However, as the Garden was planted eastward in Eden,[1] logic would say there must have been something "westward." Furthermore, when Adam and Eve were cast out of the Garden, God "placed at the east of the garden of Eden Cherubims, and a flaming sword which turned every way, to keep the way of the tree of life."[2] Therefore, while Adam and Eve were inside the Garden, there must have been something "outside," even to the east.

The major thesis of this book is that whereas the infinite Fall was absolutely necessary to our eternal progression—and is one of the three pillars of eternity[3]—being infinite, it is not bounded by time or space. We all must have agreed to Adam and Eve's role in the great plan of salvation in the grand council in heaven before the foundation of the earth (chapter 2), and it mattered not when in the course of history Adam and Eve actually lived on the earth. There is overwhelming scientific evidence that modern humans, *Homo sapiens*, have lived on Earth for around 260,000 to 350,000 years (chapters 6–8).[4] The Garden of Eden probably existed around 4000 BC, in an isolated location, away from the mainstream of humanity at the time—perhaps on the American continent (see chapter 9).

Furthermore, there is no break in the geological, biological, or anthropological record indicating any interruption in the natural progression of Earth's history—suggesting that the entire Earth went through a "paradisiacal" phase. Even if we were to find the actual, precise location of the Garden and conduct a thorough paleontological/anthropological excavation, we would almost certainly find no telltale signs of Paradise. As discussed in the previous chapter, the only things immortal in the Garden of Eden were Adam and Eve—and that because of the tree of life (to be discussed in the next chapter). Therefore, it is logical to assume that outside the Garden, while Adam and Eve were inside, life and death were going on as usual.

What about the tenth Article of Faith? "We believe . . . that the earth will be renewed and receive its paradisiacal glory." I admit, I do not know, nor do I believe anyone except God knows exactly what that scripture means in an absolute, physical sense. Furthermore, there are no other scriptures that specifically address that issue. The main problem is that we do not know what the word "renewed" means precisely. Of course the word means to restore to a "new" condition, but it is not clear precisely what Earth's condition was when it was new. I don't believe that scripture is referring to the time when the Earth was a molten sphere—or a water world. So it is not clear to what earlier time this newness refers.

When I searched for the word "paradise" in the scriptures, I found ten results: three in the New Testament, five in the Book of Mormon, and two in the Doctrine and Covenants. All three references in the New Testament are to the postmortal world. The one in Revelation is particularly interesting: "To him that overcometh will I give to eat of the tree of life, which is in the midst of the paradise of God."[5] This paradise, apparently, will exist at some future time when the Earth will become a sea of glass.[6] Is this state the condition to which the tenth Article of Faith refers? In my opinion it is.

The five references in the Book of Mormon also are all to a postmortal, spirit condition—especially preserved for the "righteous [where they] are received into a state of happiness, which is called paradise, a state of rest, a state of peace, where they shall rest from all their troubles and from all care, and sorrow."[7]

The two references in the Doctrine and Covenants, both in section 77, also refer to the postmortal world and to the conditions described in Revelation 4:6.

A search for the word "paradisiacal" brought up only one reference in the scriptures, that in the tenth Article of Faith.

Some people apparently equate paradise to lambs and lions lying down together. A search for "lamb and lion" in the scriptures yielded two in Isaiah and two in 2 Nephi (both referring to Isaiah). Isaiah 11 talks about a mighty servant of Christ, "a rod out of the stem of Jesse,"[8] who is descended from Jesse, Ephraim, and Joseph and who will begin the gathering of Israel:

> They shall not hurt nor destroy in all my holy mountain: for the earth shall be full of the knowledge of the Lord, as the waters cover the sea. And in that day there shall be a root of Jesse, which shall stand for an ensign of the people; to it shall the Gentiles seek: and his rest shall be glorious. And it shall come to pass in that day, that the Lord shall set his hand again the second time to recover the remnant of his people. . . . And he shall set up an ensign for the nations, and shall assemble the outcasts of Israel, and gather together the dispersed of Judah from the four corners of the earth.[9]

Joseph Smith fulfilled that prophecy, and an Ensign to the Nations, and the Lord's house, have been raised in the tops of the mountains, and all nations are flowing unto it.[10] In the process of that gathering, indeed, *before* the gathering spoken of above, "the wolf also shall dwell with the lamb, and the leopard shall lie down with the kid; and the calf and the young lion and the fatling together; and a little child shall lead them. And the cow and the bear shall feed; their young ones shall lie down together: and the lion shall eat straw like the ox. And the sucking child shall play on the hole of the asp, and the weaned child shall put his hand on the cockatrice' den."[11]

Because this prophecy has *already* been fulfilled, it is obvious that it is a metaphor of the peace the gospel can bring into a person's life, with the absence of strife and contention. This scripture is not talking of some future, fanciful, utopian, paradisiacal time when lions will literally be eating grass. We are also told that this prophet "shall smite the earth with the rod of his mouth, and with the breath of his lips shall he slay the wicked."[12] It is easy for us to understand this verse as metaphorical because to take it literally would be absurd.

Likewise, it is absurd not to read the lamb and lion statement as a metaphor, to believe that lions will literally eat straw like an ox—for to do so would be the assured death of the lion. Not only do lions not have grinding teeth for eating straw, even more critical, they do not have a digestive tract for digesting straw. Cattle have a ruminant stomach where bacteria can help digest the tough fibers of grass—lions do not. Cattle regurgitate the partially digested grass and then chew it again (chewing the cud)—lions cannot. Cattle have very long intestines, as much as 120 feet long, for pulling every bit of nutrition from the grasses they eat. Lions have very short intestines, only about five feet long, which can absorb large amounts of nutrients from rapidly digested meat. If a lion were to eat grass exclusively, it would die in a very short time because its intestines could not absorb enough nutrients to survive. In order for a lion to eat grass, it would have to change teeth, develop a ruminant stomach, and increase its intestines by twenty four fold—in short, it would no longer be a lion. Humans' intestines are about twenty feet long; closer to that of a lion than an ox. We can digest meat easier than grasses and we choose the seeds from grasses rather than the stems—and still we grind and cook them.

A lion literally eating grass is as absurd as a man's breath slaying the wicked. Therefore, there has never been a time in Earth's history when lions ate straw, and there never will be a time when they will eat straw. Thus, while Adam and Eve were in the Garden of Eden, the lions outside, and maybe even inside, were doing exactly what they were created to do—eating meat.

It has been my experience that some people tend to add a word to the tenth Article of Faith: "We believe . . . that the earth will be renewed and receive *again* its paradisiacal glory." This extra word apparently reflects a common belief that the entire earth was in some paradisiacal state before the Fall. There is no scriptural foundation to such a concept—as discussed in chapter 11.

NOTES

1. Genesis 2:8
2. Genesis 3:24
3. Bruce R. McConkie, BYU Speeches, Feb. 17, 1981.
4. C.M. Schlebusch, H. Malmström, T. Günther, P. Sjödin, A. Coutinho, H., Edlund, A.R. Munters, M. Vicente, M. Steyn, H. Soodyall, M. Lombard, and M. Jakobsson, "Southern Africa ancient genomes estimate

modern human divergence to 350,000 to 260,000 years ago," *Science*, 358:652–655, 2017.

5. Revelation 2:7
6. Revelation 4:6; Doctrine and Covenants 77:1
7. Alma 40:12
8. Doctrine and Covenants 113:1–6
9. Isaiah 11:9–12
10. Isaiah 2:2
11. Isaiah 11:6–8
12. Isaiah 11:4

CHAPTER 13

THE TREE OF LIFE

We are first introduced to the tree of life in the book of Genesis: "And out of the ground made the Lord God to grow . . . the tree of life also in the midst of the garden, and the tree of knowledge of good and evil."[1]

All we know at this point is that the tree of life was planted in the midst of the Garden of Eden. The account given by revelation to Moses and then to Joseph Smith gives us no additional information at this point about the tree of life.[2] The only additional information we are given in Abraham's account is the use of the plural "Gods" rather than the singular "God."[3] The book of Abraham ends before Adam and Eve's expulsion from the garden, so it provides no additional information as to the function of the tree of life.

We don't learn the function of the tree of life until after Adam and Eve had partaken of the fruit of the tree of knowledge of good and evil:

> And the Lord God said, Behold, the man is become as one of us, to know good and evil: and now, lest he put forth his hand, and take also of the tree of life, and eat, and live for ever: Therefore the Lord God sent him forth from the garden of Eden, to till the ground from whence he was taken. So he drove out the man; and he placed at the east of the garden of Eden Cherubims, and a flaming sword which turned every way, to keep the way of the tree of life.[4]

Here we learn that the reason Adam and Eve were cast out of the Garden is so that they could not "take also of the tree of life, and eat, and live for ever." We also learn that "Cherubims, and a flaming sword" were "placed at the east of the garden of Eden," but the geographic significance of such placement is not explained. Such placement may only be symbolic, with the sun rising in the east, but there may also be some other significance, which we do not know. This scripture tells us that the tree of life had the power to allow at least Adam, and presumably Eve, to live forever. It is not clear if this quality of the tree was unique to them or if anyone could become immortal by partaking of the tree of life.

The only additional information we are given in the book of Moses is the addition of one verse: "And I, the Lord God, said unto mine Only Begotten: Behold, the man is become as one of us to know good and evil; and now lest he put forth his hand and partake also of the tree of life, and eat and live forever."[5]

We are told in the book of Alma of an exchange between Alma and a chief ruler named Antionah.[6] Antionah asked Alma to explain, "What does the scripture mean, which saith that God placed cherubim and a flaming sword on the east of the garden of Eden, lest our first parents should enter and partake of the fruit of the tree of life, and live forever? And thus we see that there was no possible chance that they should live forever."[7] Alma explained:

> And now behold, I say unto you that if it had been possible for Adam to have partaken of the fruit of the tree of life at that time, there would have been no death, and the word would have been void, making God a liar, for he said: If thou eat thou shalt surely die. And we see that death comes upon mankind, yea, the death which has been spoken of by Amulek, which is the temporal death; nevertheless there was a space granted unto man in which he might repent; therefore this life became a probationary state; a time to prepare to meet God; a time to prepare for that endless state which has been spoken of by us, which is after the resurrection of the dead. . . . And now behold, if it were possible that our first parents could have gone forth and partaken of the tree of life they would have been forever miserable, having no preparatory state; and thus the plan of redemption would have been frustrated, and the word of God would have been void, taking none effect.[8]

The function of the tree of life was explained in greatest depth by Alma to his son Corianton:

> Now behold, my son, I will explain this thing unto thee. For behold, after the Lord God sent our first parents forth from the garden of Eden, to till the ground, from whence they were taken—yea, he drew out the man, and he placed at the east end of the garden of Eden,

> cherubim, and a flaming sword which turned every way, to keep the tree of life—Now, we see that the man had become as God, knowing good and evil; and lest he should put forth his hand, and take also of the tree of life, and eat and live forever, the Lord God placed cherubim and the flaming sword, that he should not partake of the fruit—And thus we see, that there was a time granted unto man to repent, yea, a probationary time, a time to repent and serve God. For behold, if Adam had put forth his hand immediately, and partaken of the tree of life, he would have lived forever, according to the word of God, having no space for repentance; yea, and also the word of God would have been void, and the great plan of salvation would have been frustrated. But behold, it was appointed unto man to die—therefore, as they were cut off from the tree of life they should be cut off from the face of the earth—and man became lost forever, yea, they became fallen man.[9]

In order to understand how a tree of life may have kept Adam and Eve alive for an indefinite period of time, it is helpful to understand why people die. As it turns out, the more we learn about our molecular biology, the more difficult that question is to answer. The more we learn, the more we understand that our cells are not necessarily destined to die, but, rather, are balanced between mortality and immortality. We seem to have a built-in mechanism for immortality, which, at present, is only partially working.

Deoxyribonucleic acid (DNA), the genetic material inside our cells, combines with specific proteins in the cell nucleus to form chromatin (*colored chemical*). During cell division, chromatin coils and condenses into chromosomes (*colored bodies*).[10] Near perfect copies of DNA are transferred from one cell generation to the next and from one human generation to the next. Our DNA sequences can be traced back thousands to millions of years—to our distant progenitors.

The problem is, the information transfer is only *nearly* perfect. Every time a cell divides, the enzymes that replicate the DNA don't quite reach the end of the DNA strands.[2] In order for DNA to replicate, the two complementary DNA strands unwind and separate. An enzyme called DNA polymerase then "reads" the DNA sequence in the two separated strands, and builds two new strands. The DNA polymerase begins the reading process with the help of short pieces of RNA. When each new strand is complete, it is a tiny fraction shorter than the original strand because of the space needed at the end for this small piece of RNA. It's a bit like painting yourself into a corner and being unable to paint the corner. As a result, the ends of each DNA molecule become a tiny bit shorter—only by a minute fraction (only about 100 bases out of 150 million bases in a typical DNA strand)—during each round of cell division. If the DNA had functioning genes at its ends, the function of those genes would eventually be lost during cell division, but "young" DNA, in a young cell, does not have functioning genes at its ends.

Telomeres (from the Greek *telos*, meaning "end," and *mero*, meaning "part") are protective end-caps on DNA molecules that help protect the DNA from replication damage. Telomeres are long, repeated sequences of the nucleotides TTAGGG, which may be repeated up to 2,500 times in newborn human cells.[2] Telomeres are somewhat like the plastic tips on shoelaces, because they keep the ends of DNA double strands from fraying and sticking to each other. Telomeres were first discovered in the mid-1970s by Elizabeth Blackburn, a postdoctoral fellow in Joseph Gall's laboratory at Yale University.[11] For her discovery, she shared the Nobel Prize in physiology and medicine with Carol Geider and Jack Szostak in 2009.

In a perfect world, our telomeres should keep our cells immortal. However, each time a cell divides, the telomeres become shorter because of that tiny gap needed for the RNA. Once the telomeres are gone, the main part of the DNA—the part with genes essential for life—starts being lost or tangled, resulting in loss of gene function. When this happens, the DNA cannot replicate completely, the ends fray, and the cell can no longer divide. That cell becomes inactive and "senescent" (old) or it dies. The telomere shortening process is associated with aging, impaired tissue repair, cancer formation, and an increased risk of death. As a result, telomeres also have been compared to the fuse on an explosive.

The telomere length in white blood cells ranges from 11,000 base pairs in newborns[12] to less than 4,000 in elderly people.[13] Each time it divides, an average cell loses 30 to 200 base pairs from the ends of its telomeres.[14] The average decline is greater in men than in women.[15] Cells normally can divide only about 50 to 70 times, with telomeres getting progressively shorter until the cells become senescent or die.

Telomere loss has been associated with some human diseases and with certain age-related changes in body functions—such as more fragile skin. Greater overall telomere loss in an individual correlates with a shorter life expectancy. Genetic variations in the proteins involved in maintaining telomeres can either raise or lower the risk and progression of certain types of cancer. Non-genetic factors, such as environmental toxins, also can affect telomere maintenance. Telomere replacement is facilitated by an enzyme called telomerase reverse transcriptase (TERT), which adds bases to the ends of telomeres.[16] In young cells, TERT is active and helps maintain telomere length. As cells divide repeatedly, however, the synthesis of TERT does not keep pace, so there is reduced telomere repair, the telomeres grow shorter, and the cells age. One key to immortality, then, is to find a way to maintain TERT synthesis at high levels. TERT synthesis is very high in sperm and egg cells, which passes high TERT activity to the next generation. If reproductive cells did not have TERT to maintain the length of their telomeres, the species would soon become extinct.

When TERT expression is enhanced in cultured cells, those cells become self-renewing, "immortal" stem cells.[17] The problem with simply increasing TERT expression is that immortal cells in the body are usually malignant cancer cells. Some cancer cells escape death by maintaining increased TERT synthesis, which prevents the telomeres from becoming shortened and allows the cell to keep dividing and become immortal.

Measuring TERT synthesis levels may be one way to detect cancer. Recent experiments have shown that if TERT activity is blocked in cancer cells growing in culture, those cells will stop dividing and die.[18] But there are risks associated with using anti-TERT therapy. Most normal cells are producing TERT and keep dividing throughout life. Therefore, blocking TERT activity could impair many normal body functions such as fertility (many anti-cancer drugs also cause birth defects), wound healing, and the production of blood cells and immune system cells.

On the other hand, finding ways to enhance TERT synthesis, while still keeping it under control, may increase longevity without producing cancer. Is it possible that telomeres and TERT hold the secret to immortality? Embryonic cells have long telomeres and high levels of TERT activity without cancer. Indeed, when cancer cells are introduced into very young embryos, those cells become normal embryonic cells. Perhaps embryos hold the secret to immortality. May we someday be able to turn adult cells into embryonic cells capable of entraining even cancer cells into normal cells? The answers to these questions are some of the most important unanswered questions in biology. Are there other keys to immortality, in addition to telomeres, yet to be discovered? The answer is yes—without question. There are already very wealthy people who have everything, except immortality, investigating techniques to extend our lives up to 1,000 years, or even more. For example, Larry Page, the Google CEO, has set up a $1.5 billion life extension research center in San Francisco called California Life Company (Calico)—and he's betting he can buy immortality.[19]

With the right knowledge, could Page, or someone else, make all the cells in the body immortal without making some of them renegade cancer cells? Is it possible that some pharmaceutical company could devise an immortality drug with no adverse side effects? The last time someone made the perfect pill with no side effects, it was called thalidomide. I've spent much of my career trying to understand what went wrong with *that* wonder drug—why it caused birth defects in thousands of children.

Maybe someone could genetically engineer the perfect tree whose fruit could keep people immortal. Maybe they'd market it as the tree of life. A study published in 2016 indicates that the antioxidants β-carotene and vitamin E in the diet can prevent telomere shortening in some cells in some people.[20] So maybe the fruit of the tree of life in the Garden of Eden contained a lot of β-carotene, vitamin E, and some other, as yet unknown, missing ingredients

Another well-known major cause of aging is oxidative stress, which causes damage to DNA, proteins, and lipids (cell membranes). Oxidants are in the air we breathe (the irony is that oxygen is one of most deadly substances to which we are exposed), in many of the foods we eat (red meat and a lot of fast foods are high in oxidants), and in other harmful substances people consume.

Antioxidants, which are abundant in fruits and vegetables, can prevent oxidative damage. Is there any fruit that can protect telomeres and be high in antioxidants? Certainly, God knows some botanical secret that even Larry Page doesn't know, despite his $1.5 billion investment. Could God have cultivated a "tree of life"? Certainly.

Black plums apparently come in first among known plants on the list of antioxidants.[21] Although I can find no scientific research concerning black plums and telomere length, I did find such a study showing that the Australian Illawarra plum *inhibits* TERT and decreases proliferation of colon cancer cells.[22] The problem this study presents is: do we stimulate TERT activity to promote immortality in all cells of the body, risking that some of those cells may become malignant, or do we want to inhibit TERT activity to inhibit immortal cancer cells, which become "immortal" independent of the other body cells?

Maybe there is some rare, exotic, nearly forgotten fruit that is the perfect antioxidant and TERT controller. How about Cupuacu, considered among the ten rarest fruits?[23] It is an Amazonian fruit rich in B vitamins, antioxidants, and other phytochemicals.[24] It apparently tastes somewhat like a pineapple or pear with a hint of banana and chocolate. Apparently, no one has yet evaluated it for its TERT-affecting ability.

Such evaluations have not yet been conducted on most fruits. As an alternative to the quest for a perfect fruit, perhaps we should find some very old people—maybe in Japan[25]—and discover what trees they have planted in their back yards. Unfortunately, I'm afraid I already know the secret to their longevity. A number of years ago, we had an exchange student from South Korea living with us. His favorite breakfast food was steamed rice, without even butter, rather than the bacon and eggs we were devouring. He also wasn't very fond of sweets. I have a difficult time envisioning paradise without bacon, eggs, caramel ice cream, and red velvet cake. I'd rather go the easy route of eating whatever I want and then occasionally consuming a little bit of fruit from the tree of life—or better yet, taking some "tree of life" pill. I wonder if we will have to diet in heaven.

NOTES

1. Genesis 2:8–9
2. Moses 3:8–9
3. Abraham 5:8–9
4. Genesis 3:22–24
5. Moses 4:28
6. Alma 12:19–29
7. Alma 12:19
8. Alma 12: 23–26
9. Alma 42: 2–6
10. R.R. Seeley, T.D. Stephens, and P. Tate, *Anatomy and Physiology*, 8th edition (Dubuque, Iowa: McGraw-Hill, 2007).

11. E.H. Blackburn and J.G. Gall, "A tandemly repeated sequence at the termini of the extrachromosomal ribosomal RNA genes in Tetrahymena," *J. Mol. Biol.,* 120: 33–53, 1978.
12. K. Okuda, A. Bardeguez, J.P. Gardner, P. Rodriguez, V. Ganesh, M. Kimura, J. Skurnick, G. Awad, and A. Aviv, "Telomere length in the newborn," *Pediatric Research,* 52: 377–381, 2002.
13. Y. Arai, C.M. Martin-Ruiz, M. Takayama, Y. Abe, T. Takebayashi, S. Koyasu, M. Suematsu, N. Hirose, and T. von Zglinicki, "Inflammation, But Not Telomere Length, Predicts Successful Ageing at Extreme Old Age: A Longitudinal Study of Semi-supercentenarians," *EBio Medicine,* 2: 1549–1548, 2015.
14. E.H. Blackburn, E.S. Epel, and J. Lin, "Human telomere biology: A contributory and interactive factor in aging, disease risks, and protection," *Science,* 350:1193–1198, 2015.
15. C. Dalgård, A. Benetos, S. Verhulst, C. Labat, J.D. Kark, K. Christensen, M. Kimura, K.O. Kyvik, and A. Aviv, "Leukocyte telomere length dynamics in women and men: menopause versus age effects," *Int J Epidemiol,* 44:1688–1695, 2015.
16. J. Shampay and E.H. Blackburn, "Generation of telomere-length heterogeneity in Saccharomyces cerevisiae," *Proc. Natl. Acad. Sci,* 85: 534–8, 1988.
17. A. Ćukušić, N. Skrobot Vidaček, M. Sopta, and I. Rubelj, "Telomerase regulation at the crossroads of cell fate," *Cytogenet. Genome Res.* 122: 263–72, 2008.
18. Z. Qi and R. Mi, "Inhibition of human telomerase reverse transcriptase in vivo and in vitro for retroviral vector-based antisense oligonucleotide therapy in ovarian cancer," *Cancer Gene Ther,* 23:36–42, 2016.
19. newsmax.com/SciTech/aging-researchers-immortality-Aubrey-de-Grey/2015/04/16
20. S. Yabuta, M. Masaki, and Y. Shidoji, "Associations of Buccal Cell Telomere Length with Daily Intake of β-Carotene or α-Tocopherol Are Dependent on Carotenoid Metabolism-related Gene Polymorphisms in Healthy Japanese Adults," *J Nutr Health Aging,* 20:267–274, 2016.
21. WebMD.com
22. E.L. Symonds, I. Konczak, I., and M. Fenech, "The Australian fruit Illawarra plum (Podocarpus elatus Endl., Podocarpaceae) inhibits telomerase, increases histone deacetylase activity and decreases proliferation of colon cancer cells," *Br J Nutr,* 109:2117–2125, 2013.
23. themysteriousworld.com
24. H. Yang, P. Protiva, B. Cui, C. Ma, S. Baggett, V. Hequet, S. Mori, I.B. Weinstein, and E.J. Kennelly, "New bioactive polyphenols from Theobroma grandiflorum ("cupuaçu")," *J Natural Products,* 66: 1501–1504, 2003.
25. Matthew Diebel, USATODAY.com, March 4, 2015.

CHAPTER 14

THE TREE OF KNOWLEDGE AND THE INFINITE FALL

We are first introduced to the tree of knowledge of good and evil at the same time we learn about the tree of life in the book of Genesis: "And out of the ground made the Lord God to grow . . . the tree of life also in the midst of the garden, and the tree of knowledge of good and evil."[1]

We are told nothing of its function in the scriptures, except that while Adam was still alone in the Garden of Eden, before Eve came on the scene, "of the tree of the knowledge of good and evil, thou shalt not eat of it: for in the day that thou eatest thereof thou shalt surely die."[2] If this verse is taken literally, at face value, it suggests that the fruit of the tree must have been poisonous—and thus a person eating the fruit would die within twenty-four hours. However, this "day" issue is cleared up in the book of Abraham account:

"But of the tree of knowledge of good and evil, thou shalt not eat of it; for in the time that thou eatest thereof, thou shalt surely die. Now I, Abraham, saw that it was after the Lord's time, which was after the time of Kolob; for as yet the Gods had not appointed unto Adam his reckoning."[3]

We are told in Facsimile 2 in the book of Abraham, "One day in Kolob is equal to a thousand years according to the measurement of this earth." It is interesting to note that, according to the scriptures, Adam died at age nine hundred and thirty.[4]

At some point, not specified, Eve was given the same instructions, either by Adam or directly by God; for we are told of her exchange with the serpent:

> And he said unto the woman: Yea, hath God said—Ye shall not eat of every tree of the garden? (And he spake by the mouth of the serpent.) And the woman said unto the serpent: We may eat of the fruit of the trees of the garden; But of the fruit of the tree which thou beholdest in the midst of the garden, God hath said—Ye shall not eat of it, neither shall ye touch it, lest ye die. And the serpent said unto the woman: Ye shall not surely die; For God doth know that in the day ye eat thereof, then your eyes shall be opened, and ye shall be as gods, knowing good and evil.[5]

Here we see in the scriptures, for the first time, a person believing Satan rather than God. But we learn from other scriptures that Eve was not entirely naive concerning the necessity of the Fall. So Eve tasted the fruit: "And when the woman saw that the tree was good for food, and that it was pleasant to the eyes, and a tree to be desired to make one wise, she took of the fruit thereof, and did eat, and gave also unto her husband with her; and he did eat."[6]

So, what exactly was the physical result of partaking of the fruit of the tree of knowledge of good and evil? We are told, "And the eyes of them both were opened, and they knew that they were naked; and they sewed fig leaves together, and made themselves aprons. And they heard the voice of the Lord God walking in the garden in the cool of the day: and Adam and his wife hid themselves from the presence of the Lord God amongst the trees of the garden."[7]

Did the fruit of the tree actually open their eyes? Or did Satan tell them that they were naked and needed to make aprons of fig leaves? "And the Lord God called unto Adam, and said unto him, Where art thou? And he said, I heard thy voice in the garden, and I was afraid, because I was naked; and I hid myself. And he said, Who told thee that thou wast naked? Hast thou eaten of the tree, whereof I commanded thee that thou shouldest not eat?"[8]

God asked Adam, "*Who told thee* that thou wast naked?" (italics added). Even though this is almost certainly a rhetorical question, it nonetheless implies that partaking of the fruit of the tree of knowledge of good and evil, *by itself,* did not instantly give Adam and Eve the notion that they were naked. We are told in Genesis 3:7 that "the eyes of them both were opened, and they knew that they were naked." But were their eyes opened in some direct physical or mental way as an immediate result of eating the forbidden fruit, or were their eyes opened because they were *told* they were naked? Outside of the temple, there is not much more that can be said of this exchange.

The stage within the Garden of Eden contained very few actors, only four that we are aware of: God, Adam, Eve, and Satan. It was obvious that neither God, nor Adam, nor Eve told them they were naked. That leaves only Satan, whom God knew was the author of their discovery of nakedness. Therefore, Adam's and Eve's eyes were opened to their nakedness, not because of some direct result of eating the fruit of the tree of knowledge, but apparently because Satan *told them* they were naked.

It is my opinion that even excluding the additional insight obtained within the temple, the exchange between God and Adam and Eve casts considerable doubt upon the hypothesis that the forbidden fruit had *any* direct, physical effect upon Adam and Eve, such as somehow magically causing their "eyes to be opened."

Furthermore, the scriptures say absolutely nothing about any other physical change coming over Adam and Eve after partaking of the fruit. There is no scripture whatsoever even remotely suggesting that some other change, such as blood entering their veins, transpired. Any such suggestion is pure speculation (the philosophies of men), has no scriptural foundation, and is contrary to all the known laws of science. This concept of blood entering their bodies after partaking of the fruit was apparently introduced to the Latter-day Saints, *de novo*, by Elder Orson Pratt in a sermon he gave in the Tabernacle in Salt Lake City, on September 11, 1859.[9] Elder Pratt had speculated about the concept as early as 1845 but had not fully articulated it at that time.[10] I have tremendous respect for Elder Pratt as one of the great early thinkers in the Church, one who was not afraid to think outside the box. However, being a great and brilliant thinker does not guarantee a person will always be correct. I think he may have been influenced, perhaps indirectly, by the writings of John Milton, as he was of the opinion that Adam and Eve were inherently immortal beings when placed on Earth.[10]

There also are no scriptures suggesting that partaking of the fruit had any effect on any other plant or animal—such as causing death to enter the world in general (the issue of 2 Nephi 2:22–23 was addressed in a previous chapter). Again, such notions are speculation, have no scriptural foundation, and again run counter to all known scientific laws. Therefore, the notion that the fruit of the tree of knowledge of good and evil contained the "seeds of death" is complete speculation, with no foundation in the scriptures or science.

A search for "tree of knowledge" in the scriptures yields only one reference in the Bible, that in Genesis 2:9, cited above. The only other references are three in the Pearl of Great Price. One each in the books of Moses and Abraham are restatements of Genesis 2:9. The third is a statement in Abraham referring to the "time" rather than the "day," as discussed above.

Searching the scriptures for the "forbidden tree" or "forbidden fruit" yielded six citations in the Book of Mormon and one in the Doctrine and Covenants. Two references in the Book of Mormon are particularly insightful. Lehi taught his son Jacob, as well as his other sons:

> And to bring about his eternal purposes in the end of man, after he had created our first parents, and the beasts of the field and the fowls of the air, and in fine, all things which are created, it must needs be that there was an opposition; even the forbidden fruit in opposition to the tree of life; the one being sweet and the other bitter. Wherefore, the Lord God gave unto man that he should act for himself. Wherefore, man could not act for himself save it should be that he was enticed by the one or the other.[11]

This scripture tells us that the tree of knowledge of good and evil was in the Garden so that Adam and Eve could "act for themselves," and they could not act for themselves unless they had a choice, and an "enticement." Here Lehi says that the fruit of the tree of knowledge was sweet, whereas that of the tree of life was bitter. This is the only time in the scriptures where the fruit of the tree of life is so described. In other places, *it* is described as sweet.

Then, in answer to a question by Antionah, a chief ruler in Ammonihah, concerning cherubim and a flaming sword guarding the tree of life, Alma stated, "Now we see that Adam did fall by the partaking of the forbidden fruit, according to the word of God; and thus we see, that by his fall, all mankind became a lost and fallen people."[12]

It is clear from this verse that the fruit of the tree of knowledge of good and evil was the very instrument of the Fall. However, the fruit of the tree of knowledge *had no apparent physiological effect* on Adam and Eve aside from "opening their eyes," which is itself debatable. As far as all other scripture is concerned, the tree of knowledge could have been any tree—an apple tree, if you will. God said to Adam and Eve, "Don't eat the fruit of that tree or you will die." It is not recorded that He told them how or why they would die if they ate the fruit.

We are told in the Doctrine and Covenants, "Wherefore, it came to pass that the devil tempted Adam, and he partook of the forbidden fruit and transgressed the commandment, wherein he became subject to the will of the devil, because he yielded unto temptation."[13]

We also read in Mosiah, "Therefore, they have drunk out of the cup of the wrath of God, which justice could no more deny unto them than it could deny that Adam should fall because of his partaking of the forbidden fruit; therefore, mercy could have claim on them no more forever."[14]

In 1845, Elder Orson Pratt made a brilliant statement concerning this event:

> It was not only the body that ate of the fruit, but the spirit gave the will to eat; the spirit sinned therefore as well as the body; they were agreed in partaking of that fruit. Was not the spirit to suffer then as well as the body? Yes. How long? To all ages of eternity, without any end; while the body was to return back to its mother earth, and there slumbered to all eternity. That was the effect of the fall, leaving out the plan of redemption; so that, if there had been no plan of redemption prepared from before the foundation of the world, man would have been subjected to an eternal dissolution of the body and spirit.[15]

Elder Dallin H. Oaks of the Quorum of the Twelve Apostles explained in the October 1993 general conference:

> For reasons that have not been revealed, this transition, or 'fall,' could not happen without a transgression—an exercise of moral agency amounting to a willful breaking of a law (see Moses 6:59). This would be a planned offense, a formality to serve an eternal purpose. . . . Lehi concludes, because "all things have been done in the wisdom of him

> who knoweth all things" (2 Nephi 2:24). . . . It was Eve who first transgressed the limits of Eden in order to initiate the conditions of mortality. Her act, whatever its nature, was formally a transgression but eternally a glorious necessity to open the doorway toward eternal life. Adam showed his wisdom by doing the same. And thus Eve and "Adam fell that men might be" (2 Nephi 2:25).
>
> Some Christians condemn Eve for her act, concluding that she and her daughters are somehow flawed by it. Not the Latter-day Saints! Informed by revelation, we celebrate Eve's act and honor her wisdom and courage in the great episode called the Fall (see Bruce R. McConkie, "Eve and the Fall," *Woman*, Salt Lake City: Deseret Book Co., 1979, pp. 67–68). Joseph Smith taught that it was not a 'sin,' because God had decreed it (see *The Words of Joseph Smith*, ed. Andrew F. Ehat and Lyndon W. Cook, Provo, Utah: Religious Studies Center, Brigham Young University, 1980, p. 63). Brigham Young declared, "We should never blame Mother Eve, not the least" (in *Journal of Discourses*, 13:145). Elder Joseph Fielding Smith said: "I never speak of the part Eve took in this fall as a sin, nor do I accuse Adam of a sin. . . . This was a transgression of the law, but not a sin . . . for it was something that Adam and Eve had to do!" (Joseph Fielding Smith, Doctrines of Salvation, comp. Bruce R. McConkie, 3 vols., Salt Lake City: Bookcraft, 1954–56, 1:114–15).[16]

Here is what actually happened, according to the scriptures, after Adam and Eve had partaken of the fruit:

> And the Lord God said, Behold, the man is become as one of us, to know good and evil: and now, lest he put forth his hand, and take also of the tree of life, and eat, and live for ever: Therefore the Lord God sent him forth from the garden of Eden, to till the ground from whence he was taken. So he drove out the man; and he placed at the east of the garden of Eden Cherubims, and a flaming sword which turned every way, to keep the way of the tree of life.[17]

God said in this scripture that man could have put forth his hand, "and take also of the tree of life, and eat, and live for ever," even *after* they had partaken of the tree of knowledge. These verses make it abundantly clear that the tree of life was the source of their immortality, and that separation from that tree would eventually bring about death. If Adam and Eve could have eaten of the tree of life and continued to live forever, it is clearly logical to conclude that after they partook of the fruit of the tree of knowledge of good and evil their bodies were still essentially the same as they had been before. Separation from the tree of life, not eating the fruit of the tree on knowledge, would eventually result in Adam and Eve's death. For Adam, that process apparently took 930 years.

This scripture also teaches that God did not drive Adam and Eve out of the Garden as a pernicious punishment but did so to isolate them from the tree of life—their source of selective immortality. We are specifically told that God "placed at the east of the garden of Eden Cherubims, and a flaming sword which turned every way, to keep the way of the tree of life." Therefore, according to this scripture, the flaming sword was not placed immediately around the tree of life, but rather, it was placed on the "way" to that tree from the east. We are told that the Garden was already "eastward,"[10] so Adam and Eve apparently went even farther east when they were driven from the Garden.

We also are given another important piece of information in these verses: "And the Lord God said, Behold, the man is become as one of us, to know good and evil."[17] First, in some way, the fruit of the tree caused, or allowed, Adam and Eve to "know good and evil." Second, knowing good and evil would in some way make Adam and Eve like "us," the Gods. This one verse provides some incredible information: first, there are *Gods*, plural, and, second, *knowledge* of good and evil is what makes them Gods.

As this verse seems to hold the very key to Godhood, it is important for us to know if this "knowledge of good and evil" was an immediate outcome of eating the fruit. According to the Bible account, God told Adam,

> Because thou hast hearkened unto the voice of thy wife, and hast eaten of the tree, of which I commanded thee, saying, Thou shalt not eat of it: cursed is the ground for thy sake; in sorrow shalt thou eat of it all the days of thy life; Thorns also and thistles shall it bring forth to thee; and thou shalt eat the herb of the field; In the sweat of thy face shalt thou eat bread, till thou return unto the ground; for out of it wast thou taken: for dust thou art, and unto dust shalt thou return. . . . Unto Adam also and to his wife did the Lord God make coats of skins, and clothed them.[18]

We are not told in Genesis how these conditions would lead Adam and Eve to a knowledge of good and evil. Genesis 3 ends with Adam and Eve being cast out of the Garden. The first verse of the next chapter states, "And Adam knew Eve his wife; and she conceived, and bare Cain, and said, I have gotten a man from the Lord."[19] There is no explanation in between as to how Adam was going to obtain a knowledge of good and evil—to become like the Gods. Furthermore, all we are told in Moses is, "Therefore I, the Lord God, will send him forth from the Garden of Eden, to till the ground from whence he was taken."[20] It appears from the above verses that eating his bread by the sweat of his face from tilling the ground was how Adam would gain a knowledge of good and evil. Other scriptures give us little additional information, so outside the temple, this is about the best we can do.

Concerning Adam and Eve's nakedness, we read in Genesis 2:25, "And they were both naked, the man and his wife, and were not ashamed." Furthermore, we are told in Genesis 3, after Adam and Eve had partaken of the forbidden fruit, about the exchange between Adam and God: "And he [Adam] said, I heard thy voice in the garden, and I was afraid, because I was naked; and I hid myself. And he [God] said, Who told thee that thou wast naked? Hast thou eaten of the tree, whereof I commanded thee that thou shouldest not eat?"[21]

Neither Abraham nor Moses gives us additional insight into this exchange. Going back to Genesis 2:25, why would Adam and Eve be ashamed of their nakedness? Before whom would they be ashamed? The only beings that they encountered in the Garden of Eden, besides themselves, were the Gods who made them in their image—God and Jesus Christ—and apparently Satan. What shame is there in having God's image? They did seem to be strongly influenced by Satan, who was a disembodied spirit. Do spirits wear clothes? Did Adam and Eve see the spirit Satan, or did they only see him as a literal serpent? Adam and Eve were husband and wife, after all.[22] Is it a shame for husband and wife to see each other's nakedness? No. It is only a shame to show *others* your nakedness.

All of 2 Nephi 2 addresses the issue of good and evil in the context of the Garden of Eden trees. In that chapter, Lehi stated, "Men are instructed sufficiently that they know good from evil."[23] From this verse we learn that *instruction* is key to knowing good from evil and, consequently, becoming as the Gods. We know that Adam and Eve received instruction both while in the Garden and after being cast out.[24] We also learn that "redemption cometh in and through the Holy Messiah"[25] and that "no flesh that can dwell in the presence of God, save it be through the merits, and mercy, and grace of the Holy Messiah."[26] We are also told that this information was part of the instructions given to Adam and Eve.[24]

Therefore, the single most important piece of *knowledge* we can obtain, allowing us to become like the Gods, is that redemption comes only through the intersession of Jesus Christ. That *knowledge* is confirmed and solidified by the Holy Ghost bearing testimony of Christ's redemption. Furthermore, we are told in Proverbs, "The fear of the Lord is the beginning of knowledge: but fools despise wisdom and instruction."[27]

Additionally, obtaining knowledge of good and evil is apparently an experiential process. Lehi continued in his address to Jacob, "For it must needs be, that there is an opposition in all things. If not so . . . righteousness could not be brought to pass, neither wickedness, neither holiness nor misery, neither good nor bad . . . having no joy, for they knew no misery; doing no good, for they knew no sin."[28] Furthermore, agency is a critical part of the process: "Wherefore, the Lord God gave unto man that he should act for himself."[29] Likewise, law also is critical to the process:

> And if ye shall say there is no law, ye shall also say there is no sin. If ye shall say there is no sin, ye shall also say there is no righteousness. And if there be no righteousness there be no happiness. And if there be no righteousness nor happiness there be no punishment nor misery. And if these things are not there is no God. And if there is no God we are not, neither the earth; for there could have been no creation of things, neither to act nor to be acted upon; wherefore, all things must have vanished away.[30]

Additionally, freedom to choose is part of the Atonement:

> And the Messiah cometh in the fulness of time, that he may redeem the children of men from the fall. And because that they are redeemed from the fall they have become free forever, knowing good from evil; to act for themselves and not to be acted upon, save it be by the punishment of the law at the great and last day, according to the commandments which God hath given. Wherefore, men are free according to the flesh; and all things are given them which are expedient unto man.

> And they are free to choose liberty and eternal life, through the great Mediator of all men, or to choose captivity and death, according to the captivity and power of the devil; for he seeketh that all men might be miserable like unto himself.[31]

Elder Orson Pratt asked, "This tree, of which they both ate, was called the tree of knowledge of good and evil. Why was it thus termed?" Then Elder Pratt gave examples of a person not appreciating sweet without ever having tasted sweet or color for a person who is blind. He then continued,

> Adam previous to partaking of this fruit; good could not be described to him, because he never had experienced the opposite. As to undertaking to explain to him what evil was, you might as well have undertaken to explain, to a being that never had . . . his eyes closed to the light, what darkness is. The tree of knowledge of good and evil was placed there that man might gain certain information he never could have been otherwise; by partaking of the forbidden fruit he experienced misery, then he knew that he was once happy, previously he could not comprehend what happiness meant, what good was; but now he knows it by contrast, now he is filled with sorrow and wretchedness, now he sees the difference between his former and present condition.[32]

Terryl and Fiona Givens stated in their 2104 book, *The Crucible of Doubt*, "It is the paradox of Eden: Eve and Adam only know what paradise is when they leave it."[33]

Paul Eastman, at the time a BYU associate professor of mechanical engineering, stated in a 2002 BYU devotional concerning the knowledge of good and evil:

> There could be no progress in becoming like God without understanding, by their own experience, the difference between good and evil.
>
> The dilemma Adam and Eve faced appears not to be a choice between good and bad. It was a choice between good things that both had unpleasant or difficult consequences. The unpleasant consequence of remaining in the Garden of Eden was that they could not become like their Father. However, choosing to experience good and evil put them in a world where there were thorns and thistles. God told them, "Because thou hast . . . eaten of the fruit of the tree . . . , cursed shall be the ground for thy sake; in sorrow shalt thou eat of it all the days of thy life" (Moses 4:23).

> Our opportunity to experience this mortal probation was a direct consequence of a correct choice in the moral dilemma Adam and Eve faced. It was a choice that our Father could not make for them without compromising their agency.
>
> A world was organized where we would have the opportunity to live and experience all of the joys and sorrows of mortality and the opportunity to experience good and evil and make choices. The challenge is recorded in Abraham 3:25: "And we will prove them herewith, to see if they will do all things whatsoever the Lord their God shall command them."[34]

In 1997, Elder Bruce C. Hafen, of the Seventy, stated,

> Life is a school, a place for us to learn and grow. We, like Adam and Eve, experience "growing pains" through the sorrow and contamination of a lone and dreary world. These experiences may include sin, but they also include mistakes, disappointments, and the undeserved pain of adversity. The blessed news of the gospel is that the atonement of Jesus Christ can purify all the uncleanness and sweeten all the bitterness we taste.[35]

The rest of the "curse" placed upon Adam and Eve is quite interesting, and may have been Israelite tradition and/or the opinion of early biblical compilers. God told Eve, "I will greatly multiply thy sorrow and thy conception; in sorrow thou shalt bring forth children; and thy desire shall be to thy husband, and he shall rule over thee."[36] Was Eve not fully female before she was cast out of the Garden? Was she not fully female in the premortal life? Had not females been giving birth to children generation upon generation for hundreds of thousands of years? Was Hannah not joyful when she bore Samuel?[37] Was Mary not joyful when she bore the Savior?[38] Jesus taught, "A woman when she is in travail hath sorrow, because her hour is come: but as soon as she is delivered of the child, she remembereth no more the anguish, for joy that a man is born into the world."[39]

And God had told Adam, "Cursed is the ground for thy sake; in sorrow shalt thou eat of it all the days of thy life; Thorns also and thistles shall it bring forth to thee; and thou shalt eat the herb of the field; In the sweat of thy face shalt thou eat bread."[40] Again, the conditions God described had been going on for millions of years. Thorns and thistles were not new to the earth, except maybe in the Garden of

Eden. But, even there, what was Adam doing when he was put there "to dress it and to keep it"[41]—that usually implies some weeding. It is almost certain that sweat was also not invented at the time of the Fall. We are told that labor brings joy: "Every man also to whom God hath given riches and wealth, and hath given him power to eat thereof, and to take his portion, and to rejoice in his labour; this is the gift of God. For he shall not much remember the days of his life; because God answereth him in the joy of his heart."[42]

We are also told, "Adam fell that men might be; and men are, that they might have joy."[43] Much like childbirth, the "sorrow" that comes with work is only short-lived and is "not much remember," with the ultimate result being joy.

The Lord said, "Wherefore, verily I say unto you that all things unto me are spiritual, and not at any time have I given unto you a law which was temporal; neither any man, nor the children of men; neither Adam, your father, whom I created."[44] Therefore, even though the tree of knowledge of good and evil was apparently a physical tree with physical fruit, the commandment was spiritual, as were the consequences of disobeying that commandment.

Because the Fall was infinite and spiritual affairs are eternal, the Fall of Adam and Eve, which opened the portal of mortality, with its school of hard knocks, and which was agreed to by all of us before the foundations of the world, could have occurred at any "time," because time itself is only a condition of our temporary, temporal existence and has no bearing or restrictions upon infinity.

NOTES

1. Genesis 2:8–9
2. Genesis 2:17
3. Abraham 5:13
4. Genesis 5:5
5. Moses 4:7–11
6. Genesis 3:6
7. Genesis 3:7–8
8. Genesis 3:9–11
9. Orson Pratt, *Journal of Discourses*, vol. 7, September 11, 1859, 254.
10. *The Orson Pratt Journals*, compiled and arranged by Elden J. Watson, published by Elden J. Watson, 1975.

11. 2 Nephi 2:15–16
12. Alma 12:22
13. Doctrine and Covenants 29:40
14. Mosiah 3:26
15. Orson Pratt, *Times and Seasons*, vol. 6, June 1, 1845, 918–20;
16. Dallin H. Oaks, "The Great Plan of Happiness," *Ensign*,Nov. 1993, 73.
17. Genesis 3:22–24
18. Genesis 3:17–19, 21
19. Genesis 4:1
20. Moses 4:29
21. Genesis 3:10–11
22. Genesis 2:24
23. 2 Nephi 2:5
24. Moses 5:4–12
25. 2 Nephi 2:6
26. 2 Nephi 2:8
27. Proverbs 1:7
28. 2 Nephi 2:11, 23
29. 2 Nephi 2:16.
30. 2 Nephi 2:13.
31. 2 Nephi 2:26–27.
32. Orson Pratt, Sermon at the Tabernacle in Salt Lake City, July 25, 1852, *Journal of Discourses,* 1:280.
33. Terryl and Fiona Givens, *The Crucible of Doubt* (Salt Lake City: Deseret Book, 2014), 34.
34. Paul F. Eastman, "The Moral Dilemma of Doing Good," *BYU Speeches*, June 25, 2002.
35. Bruce C. Hafen, "Beauty from Ashes: The Atonement of Jesus Christ," *Liahona*, April 1997.
36. Genesis 3:16
37. 1 Samuel 1:19–28
38. Luke 2:11–19
39. John 16:21
40. Genesis 3:18
41. Genesis 2:15
42. Ecclesiastes 5:19–20
43. 2 Nephi 2:25
44. Doctrine and Covenants 29:34

CHAPTER 15

CONDITIONS AFTER THE FALL

After Adam and Eve partook of the fruit of the tree of knowledge of good and evil, God said to Eve, "I will greatly multiply thy sorrow and thy conception; in sorrow thou shalt bring forth children; and thy desire shall be to thy husband, and he shall rule over thee."[1] *The Pearl of Great Price Student Manual* explains this verse of scripture:

> The Hebrew word for "multiply" is *rabah* (raw-bah), meaning to repeat over and over. It does not suggest *greater* sorrow, but rather *repeated* sorrow. The Hebrew word for "sorrow" in the Genesis account (Genesis 3:16) is from *atsab* (aw-tsab), which means "labor" or "pain." While these words suggest that toil and suffering would be a part of Eve's life, Eve did not view the conditions that came upon her through the Fall to be a curse (see Moses 5:11).[2]

We are told in Moses 5:9–10 that "the Holy Ghost fell upon Adam. . . . And in that day Adam blessed God and was filled, and began to prophesy concerning all the families of the earth, saying: Blessed be the name of God, for because of my transgression my eyes are opened, and in this life I shall have joy, and again in the flesh I shall see God."[3]

Based upon what Eve then said, it seems completely reasonable that the Holy Ghost fell upon her as well: "And Eve, his wife, heard all these things and was glad, saying: Were it not for our transgression we never should have had seed, and never should have known good and evil, and the joy of our redemption, and the eternal life which God giveth unto all the obedient."[4]

This verse tells us that Eve found gladness in her ability to have children and joy in her redemption. For most women, the pain and sorrow of childbearing is quickly swallowed up in the joy and happiness of child rearing. That joy is felt the first moment a new little baby is placed into its mother's arms.

In the October 1987 general conference of the Church, President Russell M. Nelson stated,

> Adam and Eve were joined together in marriage for time and for all eternity by the power of that everlasting priesthood (see Gen. 2:24–25; Moses 3:25; Abr. 5:18–19). Eve came as a partner, to build and to organize the bodies of mortal men. She was designed by Deity to cocreate and nurture life, that the great plan of the Father might achieve fruition. Eve "was the mother of all living" (Moses 4:26). She was the first of all women.[5]

As discussed previously, the titles "mother of all living" and "first woman" were titles of great honor and respect for Eve's place among all of God's children.

In the 1993 General Relief Society meeting held as part of general conference, Elder M. Russell Ballard, of the Quorum of the Twelve, said,

> God has revealed through his prophets that men are to receive the priesthood, become fathers, and with gentleness and pure, unfeigned love they are to lead and nurture their families in righteousness as the Savior leads the Church (see Eph. 5:23). They have been given the primary responsibility for the temporal and physical needs of the family (see D&C 83:2). Women have the power to bring children into the world and have been given the primary duty and opportunity as mothers to lead, nurture, and teach them in a loving, spiritual environment. In this divine partnership, husbands and wives support one another in their God-given capacities. By appointing different accountabilities to men and women, Heavenly Father provides the greatest opportunity for growth, service, and progress. He did not give different tasks to men and women simply to perpetuate the idea of a family; rather, He did so to ensure that the family can continue forever, the ultimate goal of our Heavenly Father's eternal plan.[6]

Concerning the phrase in Genesis 3:16 that "thy desire shall be to thy husband, and he shall rule over thee," Elder Boyd K. Packer, of the Quorum of the Twelve, stated in the October 1993 general conference:

> Should a man "exercise control or dominion or compulsion . . . in any degree of unrighteousness," . . . he violates "the oath and covenant which belongeth to the priesthood." . . . Then "the heavens withdraw themselves; the Spirit of the Lord is grieved." . . . Unless he repents he will lose his blessings.[7]

After God explained to Eve her role in bearing children, He turned His attention to Adam's condition after their expulsion from the Garden:

> Because thou hast hearkened unto the voice of thy wife, and hast eaten of the tree, of which I commanded thee, saying, Thou shalt not eat of it: cursed is the ground for thy sake; in sorrow shalt thou eat of it all the days of thy life; Thorns also and thistles shall it bring forth to thee; and thou shalt eat the herb of the field; In the sweat of thy face shalt thou eat bread, till thou return unto the ground; for out of it wast thou taken: for dust thou art, and unto dust shalt thou return. Unto Adam also and to his wife did the Lord God make coats of skins, and clothed them.[8]

President Marion G. Romney of the First Presidency taught in the 1973 October general conference,

> Now this was not a vindictive decree. The Lord was not retaliating against Adam. He was simply placing Adam in a situation where he would have to work to live. The ground was cursed in the manner prescribed for Adam's sake, not to his disadvantage. Had Adam and his posterity been able to live without working, the human race would never have survived. Idleness is pernicious.[9]

In the October 1976 general conference, President Romney taught: "Note that the curse was not placed upon Adam, but upon the ground for Adam's sake. Rather than a curse upon Adam, it was a blessing to him."[10]

In the October 2009 general conference, Elder L. Whitney Clayton of the Presidency of the Seventy stated: "Adam was told, 'Cursed shall be the ground for thy sake,' which meant for his benefit, and 'by the sweat of thy face shalt thou eat bread' (Moses 4:23, 25). Work is a continual burden, but it is also a continual blessing 'for [our] sake,' for it teaches lessons *we* can learn only 'by the sweat of [our] face.'"[11]

The American Tract Society Bible Dictionary states for thorns and thistles, "Under these terms, together with brambles, briers, and nettles, are included numerous troublesome plants, many of them with thorns, well fitted to try the husbandman's patience."[12] *Strong's Hebrew Dictionary of the Bible* equates thistle to briar.[12]

The name "thistle" is commonly given to flowering plants, often of the aster, daisy, and sunflower families, with small thorns on their leaves and stems. A thorn is a stiff, sharp-pointed fibrous projection on a plant. The term "thorn" may also apply to a specific bush or tree. Most people consider thistles to be highly undesirable weeds—unless you live in Scotland where thistles are the national symbol and people cultivate numerous varieties in their gardens.

Some of the oldest land plants, such as the *Drepanophycus* of the Devonian age (420 to 370 million years ago), were covered with spines or thorns.[13] There are pollen and seeds from the Asteraceae family, to which many thistles belong, occurring in Oligocene deposits from around 33.9 million to 23 million years ago.[14] So, clearly, thorns and thistles existed in the outside world, long before Adam and Eve left the Garden. It may be that, being isolated within the Garden, they had never encountered such plants, at least to their recollection.

The book of Moses provides much more detail than does Genesis concerning the conditions into which Adam and Eve were placed after they left Eden: "And it came to pass that after I, the Lord God, had driven them out, that Adam began to till the earth, and to have dominion over all the beasts of the field, and to eat his bread by the sweat of his brow, as I the Lord had commanded him. And Eve, also, his wife, did labor with him."[15]

Tilling the earth suggests agriculture, and the earliest agriculture so far discovered began around 11,500 years ago with eight "founder crops": emmer, einkorn wheat, bitter vetch, barley, flax, lentils, peas, and chick peas; mainly in what is now Syria—some 5,500 years before Adam.[16] Fig trees were first cultivated around the same time.[17] Rice was first domesticated in China around 8,200–13,500 years ago.[18] Plants were not domesticated in a single generation but required many generations of selective breeding to obtain suitable plants with suitable growth and high yields. Furthermore, agriculture involves a very sophisticated set of skills, not developed by a single individual. Was part of the "knowledge" obtained by Adam taught to him by someone who had been employing agriculture over a considerable period of time?

God commanded Adam and Eve "that they should . . . offer the firstlings of their flocks, for an offering unto the Lord."[19] "Their flocks" suggested that Adam and Eve also had domesticated animals. Ancient domestication of animals has been identified in at least eleven separate, independent places in both the Old and New Worlds.[20] Wild boars were changed into domestic pigs in Europe and Asia around 10,500 years ago.[21] Sheep and goats were domesticated just north of the fertile crescent around 11,000 to 13,000 years ago.[22] Wild aurochs were domesticated into cattle in Turkey and Pakistan around 10,500 years ago.[23]

The term "flocks" specifically suggests that Adam and Eve were herding domestic sheep and/or goats. Domestication does not occur immediately but requires many generations of animals. It is very likely that Adam and Eve emerged into a society where domestic sheep and goats had already been around for several thousand years.

One problem concerning Adam and Eve's connection to agriculture is that all of the grains and domestic animals listed above were domesticated in Eurasia and none came to the Americas until after 1492. The only sheep known to anthropology before that date in the Americas were the wild sheep of the Rocky Mountains, which apparently have never been domesticated. So there is an unanswered question as to *what* was being sacrificed by Adam and his descendants or *where* were those sacrifices taking place. As discussed in chapter 9, the location of the Garden of Eden and Adam-ondi-Ahman to North America in general and Spring Hill, Missouri, in particular is somewhat ambiguous in modern scripture, even though Joseph Smith seems to have been quite convinced that the Garden of Eden was in Missouri. The agrarian nature of Adam's post-garden experience suggests that the stage was the Middle East. Therefore, Adam-ondi-Ahman may be a general name, such that Adam's meeting shortly before his death was in the Middle East[24] but the later meeting, at Christ's return, is to be in Missouri.[25]

In similar fashion, the Pilgrims, who first came to Massachusetts, named their colony Plymouth, after the port in England from which they sailed. It has been a common practice throughout human history to give the same name to multiple places. This paradox of whether there was one or two Adam-ondi-Ahmans, and what domestic plants and animals Adam encountered, I believe, will remain unresolved until additional revelation clarifies this specific period in history. I, personally, am not going to stake my faith on this one point of minutia when there is so much more to the gospel than this one issue.

Wherever the story of Adam and Eve was played out, the narrative continues. We are then told in the book of Moses, "And Adam and Eve, his wife, called upon the name of the Lord."[26]

NOTES

1. Genesis 3:16; Moses 4:22
2. *The Pearl of Great Price Student Manual*, 2017.
3. Moses 5:9–10
4. Moses 5:11
5. Russell M. Nelson, "Lessons from Eve," October 1987 general conference.
6. M. Russell Ballard, *Ensign,* Nov. 1993, 90.
7. Boyd K. Packer, *Ensign,* Nov. 1993, 22.
8. Genesis 3:17–19, 21; Moses 4:23–25
9. Marion G. Romney, "Church Welfare—Some Fundamentals," October 1973 general conference.
10. Marion G. Romney, "In Mine Own Way," October 1976 general conference.
11. L. Whitney Clayton, "That Your Burdens May Be Light," October 2009 general conference.
12. biblehub.com/topical/t/thistles_and_thorns.htm
13. W.N. Stewart and G.W. Rothwell, *Paleobotany and the evolution of plants*, second edition (Cambridge: Cambridge University Press, 1993).
14. K. Bremer and M.H.G. Gustafsson, "East Gondwana ancestry of the sunflower alliance of families," *Proc. Natl. Acad. Sci.*, U.S., 94:9188–9190, 1997.
15. Moses 5:1
16. K. Kris Hirst, "The Eight Founder Crops and the Origins of Agriculture," thoughtco.com/founder-crops-origins-of-agriculture-171203, 2017.
17. Mordechai E. Kislev, Anat Hartmann, and Ofer Bar-Yosef, "Early Domesticated Fig in the Jordan Valley," *Science*, 312:1372–1374, 2006.
18. ricepedia.org/culture/history-of-rice-cultivation
19. Moses 5:5

20. G. Larson, et al., "Current perspectives and the future of domestication studies," *Proc. Natl. Acad. Sci.*, 111:6139, 2014.
21. Greger Larson, et al., "Ancient DNA, pig domestication, and the spread of the Neolithic into Europe," *Proc. Natl. Acad. Sci.*, 104:15276–15281, 2007
22. M.E. Ensminger and R.O. Parker, *Sheep and Goat Science*, Fifth ed., (Danville, IL: Interstate Printers and Publishers, 1986).
23. E.J. McTavish, J.E. Decker, R.D. Schnabel, J.F. Taylor, and D.M. Hillis, "New world cattle show ancestry from multiple independent domestication events," *Proc. Natl. Acad. Sci.*, 110:1398–406, 2013.
24. Doctrine and Covenants 107:53
25. Doctrine and Covenants 116:1
26. Moses 5:4

CHAPTER 16

ADAM AND EVE'S FAMILY

Genesis 3 ends with Adam and Eve being driven out of the Garden of Eden. Chapter 4 opens immediately with the birth of Cain: "And Adam knew Eve his wife; and she conceived, and bare Cain, and said, I have gotten a man from the Lord. And she again bare his brother Abel. And Abel was a keeper of sheep, but Cain was a tiller of the ground."[1]

We will discuss the story of Cain and Abel in the next chapter. Here we see that the book of Genesis goes on with the story of Adam's family after Abel's death: "And Adam knew his wife again; and she bare a son, and called his name Seth. For God, said she, hath appointed me another seed instead of Abel, whom Cain slew. And to Seth, to him also there was born a son; and he called his name Enos: then began men to call upon the name of the Lord."[2]

The book of Moses provides much more detail about what happened after the Fall. In particular, that account does not place Cain as the firstborn of Adam and Eve. We are informed:

> And it came to pass that after I, the Lord God, had driven them out, that Adam began to till the earth, and to have dominion over all the beasts of the field, and to eat his bread by the sweat of his brow, as I the Lord had commanded him. And Eve, also, his wife, did labor with him. And Adam knew his wife, and she bare unto him sons and daughters, and they began to multiply and to replenish the earth. And from that time forth, the sons and daughters of Adam began to divide two and two in the land, and to till the land, and to tend flocks, and they also begat sons and daughters.[3]

Again, as discussed in the previous chapter, it is clear from both accounts that the children of Adam and Eve were involved in agricultural practices "to till the land" and "to tend flocks." According to the New American Standard Lexicon, the Hebrew word דָבַע (*oved*), which was translated in the King James Bible as "till," actually means to work, or to serve, and the Hebrew word הָמָדְא: (*adamah,* the same root as Adam) means ground or land.[4] The choice of the word "till" in the King James Bible is probably too modern of a term, and the word "work" or "serve" would probably have been a better choice. According to Merriam-Webster, "till" comes from twelfth century Old English *tilian* (meaning good or suitable) and means "to turn, break up, or work with a plow," to make the land "good" or "suitable" for growing crops. Furthermore, a plow is "an implement used to cut, lift, and turn over soil especially in preparing a seedbed."[5]

Tilling of any kind, even in the earliest times, suggests the use of implements. The most primitive tilling implement is a digging stick,[6] which makes a single hole for planting, was probably used from the dawn of agriculture some 11,500 years ago,[7] was probably independently invented numerous times around the world, and is still used in some parts of the world today. Because digging sticks had been available for over 5,000 years before Adam, and were simple inventions, this form of tilling would likely have been used by Adam, Eve, and their children.

Oxen were first domesticated in Mesopotamia and the Indus Valley over 7,000 years ago—perhaps 1,000 years before Adam—and such animals could pull an ard (or scratch plow). However, the use of such animals for deeper plowing apparently did not occur until a couple thousand years later. The oldest plowed fields so far found on earth were discovered in the Indus Valley civilization site of Kalibangan, dating to about 4,800 years ago—around 1,200 years after Adam.[8] By around 4,000 years ago, the practice of using cattle for plowing had appeared in Egypt.[9] Therefore, whatever tilling that was accomplished by Adam's family was apparently done by hand.

The book of Moses tells us that Adam and Eve had multiple children, perhaps numerous children, "who began to divide two and two in the land . . . begat sons and daughters."[10] We also read:

> Adam and Eve, his wife, called upon the name of the Lord, and they heard the voice of the Lord from the way toward the Garden of Eden, speaking unto them, and they saw him not; for they were shut out from his presence. And he gave unto them commandments, that they should worship the Lord their God, and should offer the firstlings of their flocks, for an offering unto the Lord. And Adam was obedient unto the commandments of the Lord.[11]

Adam was taught the great plan of salvation and about the role of sacrifice in foretelling Christ's Atonement.

> And after many days an angel of the Lord appeared unto Adam, saying: Why dost thou offer sacrifices unto the Lord? And Adam said unto him: I know not, save the Lord commanded me. And then the angel spake, saying: This thing is a similitude of the sacrifice of the Only Begotten of the Father, which is full of grace and truth. Wherefore, thou shalt do all that thou doest in the name of the Son, and thou shalt repent and call upon God in the name of the Son forevermore.[12]

So, from early on after their expulsion from the Garden, Adam and Eve were taught about the mission of Jesus Christ and His Atonement. It is significant that even though they walked and talked with Him while they were in the Garden, the significance of His Atonement would not have meant anything to them until after the Fall. Furthermore, had Adam and Eve known of the redemption while they were in the Garden, their test in abstaining from the forbidden fruit would not have been so much of a test. Likewise with us, we are not given to see the long-range consequences of our choices while we are in the midst of being tested. After Adam and Eve had obeyed the commandment to make sacrifices, the following happened:

> And in that day the Holy Ghost fell upon Adam, which beareth record of the Father and the Son, saying: I am the Only Begotten of the Father from the beginning, henceforth and forever, that as thou hast fallen thou mayest be redeemed, and all mankind, even as many as will. And in that day Adam blessed God and was filled, and began to prophesy concerning all the families of the earth, saying: Blessed be the name of God, for because of my transgression my eyes are opened, and in this life I shall have joy, and again in the flesh I shall see God. And Eve, his wife, heard all these things and was glad, saying: Were it not for our transgression we never should have had seed, and never

> should have known good and evil, and the joy of our redemption, and the eternal life which God giveth unto all the obedient. And Adam and Eve blessed the name of God, and they made all things known unto their sons and their daughters. . . . And the Lord God called upon men by the Holy Ghost everywhere and commanded them that they should repent; And as many as believed in the Son, and repented of their sins, should be saved; and as many as believed not and repented not, should be damned; and the words went forth out of the mouth of God in a firm decree; wherefore they must be fulfilled. And Adam and Eve, his wife, ceased not to call upon God.[13]

The statement that "God called upon men . . . *everywhere* and commanded them that they should repent" suggests that there were more people than just Adam's family on Earth and that they were already dispersed *everywhere.*

Genesis 5 begins with all the "begats":

> This is the book of the generations of Adam. In the day that God created man, in the likeness of God made he him; Male and female created he them; and blessed them, and called their name Adam, in the day when they were created. And Adam lived an hundred and thirty years, and begat a son in his own likeness, after his image; and called his name Seth: And the days of Adam after he had begotten Seth were eight hundred years: and he begat sons and daughters: And all the days that Adam lived were nine hundred and thirty years: and he died.[14]

Chapter 5 continues with a list of some very old men with their ages given in extraordinary detail. There are no archeological data, of which I am aware, suggesting any time in the history of the world when the general population lived to extremely old ages. Indeed, as far as we know, from the available data, we currently have the longest life expectancies of any people who have ever lived on earth. Nonetheless, according to both the Bible and the Pearl of Great Price, for nine generations, from Adam to Lamech, the patriarchs lived to very old ages. Methuselah held the record at 969 years.[15] No mention is made of how long the women or any other people lived. Indeed, the fact that their ages are listed so precisely suggests that their ages were anomalies, even among their peers.

There are several possible explanations for the ages presented, which are exactly the same in Genesis and Moses. One possibility is that age was calculated differently in those days. If this were the case, however, why would the scriptures put so much emphasis on the ages of nine men? Another possibility is that these are in some way "heroic" ages, much in the same way that Celtic heroes were all literally bigger than life—larger than other humans of their time. Third, maybe they continued on some sort of high-level antioxidant diet, although not as good as that provided by the tree of life. A fourth possibility is that those nine men inherited some aspect of Adam's longevity. Perhaps they inherited extra-long telomeres or more active, or a greater number of telomerases.

Richard Cawthon and colleagues at the University of Utah proposed that there are four possible components to aging: telomere shortening, chronological age, oxidative stress, and glycation (binding of glucose—sugar—to DNA, proteins, and lipids). Cawthon and his team proposed that if we could eliminate the majority of the aging processes, such as telomere shortening and glycation, and figure out how to repair oxidative damage, humans could live to be as much as 1,000 years old—older than Methuselah.[16]

We are told in Doctrine and Covenants 107 that Adam personally ordained many of his descendants to the priesthood.

> Seth . . . was ordained by Adam at the age of sixty-nine years . . . Enos was ordained at the age of one hundred and thirty-four years and four months, by the hand of Adam . . . God called upon Cainan in the wilderness in the fortieth year of his age; and he met Adam in journeying to the place Shedolamak. He was eighty-seven years old when he received his ordination. Mahalaleel was four hundred and ninety-six years and seven days old when he was ordained by the hand of Adam, who also blessed him . . . Enoch was twenty-five years old when he was ordained under the hand of Adam; and he was sixty-five and Adam blessed him . . . Methuselah was one hundred years old when he was ordained under the hand of Adam.[17]

Adam also called his family together shortly before his death and gave them blessings.

> Three years previous to the death of Adam, he called Seth, Enos, Cainan, Mahalaleel, Jared, Enoch, and Methuselah, who were all high priests, with the residue of his posterity who were righteous, into the valley of Adam-ondi-Ahman, and there bestowed upon them his last

> blessing. And Adam stood up in the midst of the congregation; and, notwithstanding he was bowed down with age, being full of the Holy Ghost, predicted whatsoever should befall his posterity unto the latest generation.[18]

We are also promised in the Doctrine and Covenants that Adam will come to Adam-ondi-Ahman in the last days: "Spring Hill is named by the Lord Adam-ondi-Ahman, because, said he, it is the place where Adam shall come to visit his people, or the Ancient of Days shall sit, as spoken of by Daniel the prophet."[19]

In Daniel we read, "Until the Ancient of days came, and judgment was given to the saints of the most High; and the time came that the saints possessed the kingdom."[20]

And, again, we read in the Doctrine and Covenants:

> Behold, this is wisdom in me; wherefore, marvel not, for the hour cometh that I will drink of the fruit of the vine with you on the earth, and with Moroni, whom I have sent unto you to reveal the Book of Mormon, containing the fulness of my everlasting gospel, to whom I have committed the keys of the record of the stick of Ephraim. . . . And also with Michael, or Adam, the father of all, the prince of all, the ancient of days.[21]

In 1867, Elder George Q. Cannon, commented about this place, Adam-ondi-Ahman, and the meeting to occur there:

> We look forward to that land [Missouri] with indescribable feelings, because it is the place where God has said His City shall be built. It is the land where Adam, the Ancient of Days, will gather his posterity again, and where the blessings of God will descend upon them. . . . God in His revelations has informed us that it was on this choice land of Joseph where Adam was placed and the Garden of Eden was laid out. The spot has been designated, and we look forward with peculiar feelings to repossessing that land. We expect when that day shall come that we will be a very different people to what we are today. We will be prepared to commune with heavenly beings; at any rate, the preparation will be going on very rapidly for Jesus to be revealed. We expect that a society will be organized there that will be a pattern of heavenly society, that when Jesus and the heavenly beings who come with him are revealed in the clouds of heaven, their feelings will not be shocked by the change, for a society will be organized on the earth whose members will be prepared through the revelations of God to

> meet and associate with them, if not on terms of perfect equality, at least with some degree of equality.[22]

One hundred fifty one years later, in the Sunday morning session of the April 2018 general conference, President Russell M. Nelson invited us to follow the very plan to become "a very different people to what we are today," as predicted by Elder Cannon:

> One of the things the Spirit has repeatedly impressed upon my mind since my new calling as President of the Church is how willing the Lord is to reveal His mind and will. The privilege of receiving revelation is one of the greatest gifts of God to His children. . . . If we will truly receive the Holy Ghost and learn to discern and understand His promptings, we will be guided in matters large and small.
>
> Pray in the name of Jesus Christ about your concerns, your fears, your weaknesses—yes, the very longings of your heart. And then listen! Write the thoughts that come to your mind. Record your feelings and follow through with actions that you are prompted to take. As you repeat this process day after day, month after month, year after year, you will "grow into the principle of revelation."
>
> Does God really *want* to speak to you? Yes! . . . I urge you to stretch beyond your current spiritual ability to receive personal revelation, for the Lord has promised that "if thou shalt [seek], thou shalt receive revelation upon revelation, knowledge upon knowledge, that thou mayest know the mysteries and peaceable things—that which bringeth joy, that which bringeth life eternal.
>
> Oh, there is so much more that your Father in Heaven wants you to know. As Elder Neal A. Maxwell taught, "To those who have eyes to see and ears to hear, it is clear that the Father and the Son are giving away the secrets of the universe!"
>
> Nothing opens the heavens quite like the combination of increased purity, exact obedience, earnest seeking, daily feasting on the words of Christ in the Book of Mormon, and regular time committed to temple and family history work. . . . But I promise that as you continue to be obedient, expressing gratitude for every blessing the Lord gives you, and as you patiently honor the Lord's timetable, you will be given the knowledge and understanding you seek. Every blessing the Lord has for you—even miracles—will follow. That is what personal revelation will do for you.
>
> Our Savior and Redeemer, Jesus Christ, will perform some of His mightiest works between now and when He comes again. . . . My beloved brothers and sisters, I plead with you to increase your spiritual capacity

to receive revelation. . . . Choose to do the spiritual work required to enjoy the gift of the Holy Ghost and hear the voice of the Spirit more frequently and more clearly.[23]

NOTES

1. Genesis 4:1–2
2. Genesis 4:25–26
3. Moses 5:1–3
4. New American Standard Bible (NASB) Lexicon; biblehub.com/lexicon/genesis/4–2.
5. merriam-webster.com/dictionary/till
6. J. Rios-Garaizar, O. López-Bultó, E. Iriarte, C. Pérez-Garrido, R. Piqué, A. Aranburu, et al., *A Middle Palaeolithic wooden digging stick from Aranbaltza III*, Spain, *PLoS ONE* 13(3): e0195044; doi.org/10.1371/journal.pone.0195044, 2018.
7. K. Kris Hirst, "The Eight Founder Crops and the Origins of Agriculture," thoughtco.com/founder-crops-origins-of-agriculture-171203, 2017.
8. B.B. Lal, "Excavations at Kalibangan, the Early Harappans, 1960–1969," *Archaeological Survey of India*, 2003, 17, 98.
9. Geraldine Woods, *Science in Ancient Egypt* (New York, NY: Watts, 1988).
10. Moses 5:3
11. Moses 5:4–5
12. Moses 5:6–8
13. Moses 5:9–16
14. Genesis 5:1–5
15. Genesis 5:27
16. Richard Cawthon, University of Utah Genetic Science Learning Center, learn.genetic.utah.edu.
17. Doctrine and Covenants 107:42–50
18. Doctrine and Covenants 107:53, 56
19. Doctrine and Covenants 116:1
20. Daniel 7:22
21. Doctrine and Covenants 27:5, 11
22. George Q. Cannon, discourse delivered in the Tabernacle, Salt Lake City, March 3, 1867, as reported by David W. Evans, *Journal of Discourses*, 11:330–339 (Liverpool, 1867); Exact Photo Reprint, 1966.
23. Russell M. Nelson, "Revelation for the Church, Revelation for Our Lives," April 2018 general conference.

CHAPTER 17

CAIN AND ABEL

Even though Adam and Eve taught their children the revelations they received from God and the commandments they had been given, their children preferred to follow Satan rather than God: "And Satan came among them, saying: I am also a son of God; and he commanded them, saying: Believe it not; and they believed it not, and they loved Satan more than God. And men began from that time forth to be carnal, sensual, and devilish."[1]

In the Garden of Eden, "Satan put it into the heart of the serpent, (for he had drawn away many after him,) . . . to beguile Eve."[2] Why did Satan use the mouth of a serpent in the Garden of Eden to speak to Eve? Could he not speak for himself? He was, after all, only a disembodied spirit (although this part of the story may be allegorical). Likewise, we might suppose that when Satan came among the children of Adam, he may also have used some other's mouth to do his enticing, for he had already "drawn away many after him."[2] How could Satan have drawn many away when Adam and Eve were the only ones present? Of course, this scripture could have reference to the premortal life, but then why put the phrase in parentheses right after the serpent? It is my opinion that Satan does not have direct access to God's children but comes among us by indirect methods such as the enticings of the world.

It also is my opinion that when Adam and Eve stepped out of their isolation in the Garden of Eden into the lone and dreary world, they did not step into an empty world. I believe the word "lone" means that they were without their previous association with God. Today, we can feel that same sense of loneliness, even on a crowded city street, if we separate ourselves from God's presence through our transgressions.

The account of Adam's family in Genesis and Moses suggests that Adam, Eve, and their children were the only human beings on Earth six thousand years ago. A conservative estimate for the number of people living on Earth at that time, however, is seven million.[3] How do we account for the discrepancy? One answer is that, although there were seven million people on Earth, Adam and his family were isolated from the rest of humanity. An alternative answer is that Adam and his family were not alone. There are a number of hints in the scriptures that the latter might be the case.

It is likely that Satan used other humans, whom he had already led astray, surrounding Adam and Eve's children and grandchildren to lead them away from their parents' teachings. Alternatively, although we don't at present know why, one way in which Adam was the first man was that he was the first human on Earth to be visited by God, the first to be touched by the Holy Ghost, the first to be baptized, and the first to receive the holy priesthood. Why would God allow generation upon generation of His children to pass away without those blessings? We are not fully told, except that we know all of God's children will ultimately have the opportunity to accept God's plan and the Savior's redemption. We may ask equally, why were generation upon generation of His children allowed to pass away without those blessings before Abraham's covenant or between the Apostasy and the Restoration? We are simply not told. I believe that all those who came before Adam as well as all those who lived throughout all generations without access to the priesthood, attended, along with us, that grand council in heaven where the complete plan was unfolded. I believe that their parts in the plan were explained and that they accepted their foreordained roles. I believe that they all understood that whatever their assigned time and conditions on Earth, we are all partakers of Adam's part in that great plan as well as Christ's loving redemption of all mankind.

> And the Lord God called upon men by the Holy Ghost everywhere and commanded them that they should repent; And as many

> as believed in the Son, and repented of their sins, should be saved; and as many as believed not and repented not, should be damned; and the words went forth out of the mouth of God in a firm decree; wherefore they must be fulfilled.[4]

When Enoch was teaching the posterity of Adam, he went into great detail describing a conversation between God and Adam about the Atonement, repentance and baptism. Enoch's recounting of that conversation occupies Moses 6:51–68. Only a portion is quoted here:

> If thou wilt turn unto me, and hearken unto my voice, and believe, and repent of all thy transgressions, and be baptized, even in water, in the name of mine Only Begotten Son, who is full of grace and truth, which is Jesus Christ, the only name which shall be given under heaven, whereby salvation shall come unto the children of men, ye shall receive the gift of the Holy Ghost, asking all things in his name, and whatsoever ye shall ask, it shall be given you.
>
> And our father Adam spake unto the Lord, and said: Why is it that men must repent and be baptized in water? And the Lord said unto Adam...That by reason of transgression cometh the fall, which fall bringeth death, and inasmuch as ye were born into the world by water, and blood, and the spirit, which I have made, and so became of dust a living soul, even so ye must be born again into the kingdom of heaven, of water, and of the Spirit, and be cleansed by blood, even the blood of mine Only Begotten; that ye might be sanctified from all sin, and enjoy the words of eternal life in this world, and eternal life in the world to come, even immortal glory; For by the water ye keep the commandment; by the Spirit ye are justified, and by the blood ye are sanctified... This is the plan of salvation unto all men, through the blood of mine Only Begotten, who shall come in the meridian of time.
>
> And it came to pass, when the Lord had spoken with Adam, our father, that Adam cried unto the Lord, and he was caught away by the Spirit of the Lord, and was carried down into the water, and was laid under the water, and was brought forth out of the water. And thus he was baptized, and the Spirit of God descended upon him, and thus he was born of the Spirit, and became quickened in the inner man.[5]

Paradoxically, Adam's acceptance of the Savior, Jesus Christ, and his subsequent baptism placed him, Adam, under the Abrahamic covenant.[6] Therefore, Adam would be counted as Abraham's seed, even though the latter would not be born for another two thousand years.

This apparent paradox emphasizes the *infinite* nature of gospel covenants and why temporal considerations, such as "first man," have no meaning in such a context.

We next come to the story of Cain and Abel in the books of Genesis and Moses. I will use the Moses account as being the most complete.

> And Adam and Eve, his wife, ceased not to call upon God. And Adam knew Eve his wife, and she conceived and bare Cain, and said: I have gotten a man from the Lord; wherefore he may not reject his words. But behold, Cain hearkened not, saying: Who is the Lord that I should know him?[7]

This statement by Cain is the very essence of pride and demonstrates a complete lack of meekness and humility. It seems that in spite of parents' best efforts to teach our children about God and to follow Him, some of our children pridefully use their free agency and turn away from Him and us. We are told in the book of Mosiah,

> For the natural man is an enemy to God, and has been from the fall of Adam, and will be, forever and ever, unless he yields to the enticings of the Holy Spirit, and putteth off the natural man and becometh a saint through the atonement of Christ the Lord, and becometh as a child, submissive, meek, humble, patient, full of love, willing to submit to all things which the Lord seeth fit to inflict upon him, even as a child doth submit to his father.[8]

We also are told in the book of Helaman:

> And thus we can behold how false, and also the unsteadiness of the hearts of the children of men. . . . O how foolish, and how vain, and how evil, and devilish, and how quick to do iniquity, and how slow to do good, are the children of men; yea, how quick to hearken unto the words of the evil one, and to set their hearts upon the vain things of the world! Yea, how quick to be lifted up in pride; yea, how quick to boast, and do all manner of that which is iniquity; and how slow are they to remember the Lord their God, and to give ear unto his counsels, yea, how slow to walk in wisdom's paths![9]

The story of Cain and Abel continues in a developed Middle-eastern agricultural setting: "And she again conceived and bare his brother Abel. And Abel hearkened unto the voice of the Lord. And Abel was a keeper of sheep, but Cain was a tiller of the ground."[10]

Then comes the key part of the story, the offering of sacrifice. Adam and Eve had been commanded to "offer the firstlings of their flocks . . . [in] similitude of the sacrifice of the Only Begotten of the Father."[11] No other offering, such as "the fruit of the ground," would be acceptable because it would not represent the blood of the "Only Begotten of the Father." We are told:

> And Cain loved Satan more than God. And Satan commanded him, saying: Make an offering unto the Lord. And in process of time it came to pass that Cain brought of the fruit of the ground an offering unto the Lord. And Abel, he also brought of the firstlings of his flock, and of the fat thereof. And the Lord had respect unto Abel, and to his offering; But unto Cain, and to his offering, he had not respect. Now Satan knew this, and it pleased him. And Cain was very wroth, and his countenance fell.
>
> And the Lord said unto Cain: Why art thou wroth? Why is thy countenance fallen? If thou doest well, thou shalt be accepted. And if thou doest not well, sin lieth at the door, and Satan desireth to have thee; and except thou shalt hearken unto my commandments, I will deliver thee up, and it shall be unto thee according to his desire. And thou shalt rule over him.[12]

According to 2 Nephi 9:9 and 2 Corinthians 11:14, Satan transformed himself into "an angel of light" when he "stirreth up the children of men unto secret combinations of murder and all manner of secret works of darkness."[13] When "the Lord said unto Cain," was He speaking directly to Cain, or was He speaking through Adam? We are told in Moses 5:4 that Adam and Eve heard God's voice back toward the Garden of Eden, but we are not told that God spoke directly to any of their children. Indeed, the first portion of Moses 5 would suggest otherwise—that God's words were passed from Adam and Eve to their children. The first part of the second paragraph quoted above is very similar to modern revelations give to various people through the Prophet Joseph Smith.[14] Furthermore, the last portion of the scripture, "And thou shalt rule over him," may not be unique to Cain.

In a December 1976 *Ensign* article, Hugh Nibley, Professor Emeritus of Ancient Scripture at Brigham Young University, addressed this issue:

> Cain rule over Satan? Yes, that is the arrangement—the devil serves his client, gratifies his slightest whim, pampers his appetites,

> and is at his beck and call throughout his earthly life, putting unlimited power and influence at his disposal through his command of the treasures of the earth, gold and silver. But in exchange the victim must keep his part of the agreement, following Satan's instructions on earth and remaining in his power hereafter. That is the classic bargain, the pact with the Devil, by which a Faust, Don Juan, Macbeth, or Jabez Stone achieve the pinnacle of earthly success and the depths of eternal damnation.[15]

But Cain's connection to Satan and the works of darkness apparently go way beyond any pact with the devil that ever occurred in times since—none but Cain was given the name Perdition. These were still God's warnings to Cain, and He gave Cain one last chance:

> For from this time forth thou shalt be the father of his lies; thou shalt be called Perdition; for thou wast also before the world. And it shall be said in time to come—That these abominations were had from Cain; for he rejected the greater counsel which was had from God; and this is a cursing which I will put upon thee, except thou repent.[16]

Was this admonition to Cain given from God directly or from God through Adam? This condemnation of Cain is reminiscent of Lehi's concern over Laman and Lemuel following his vision of the tree of life.

> And it came to pass after my father had spoken all the words of his dream or vision, which were many, he said unto us, because of these things which he saw in a vision, he exceedingly feared for Laman and Lemuel; yea, he feared lest they should be cast off from the presence of the Lord.[17]

Nonetheless, as with the case for Laman and Lemuel many years later, Cain refused to listen to God, or to his father and mother:

> And Cain was wroth, and listened not any more to the voice of the Lord, neither to Abel, his brother, who walked in holiness before the Lord. And Adam and his wife mourned before the Lord, because of Cain and his brethren.[18]

Much like the story of Nephi and his brothers, Laman and Lemuel, the above verses indicate that Abel also attempted to convince Cain to follow God's commandments and warnings. But like the later story of Laman and Lemuel, and the daughters of Ishmael, "And it came to pass that Cain took one of his brothers' daughters to wife, and they loved Satan more than God."[19] This seems to be a recurring story, of entire families torn apart by this conflict between God and Satan. And Cain moved even further into Satan's control:

> And Satan said unto Cain: Swear unto me by thy throat, and if thou tell it thou shalt die; and swear thy brethren by their heads, and by the living God, that they tell it not; for if they tell it, they shall surely die; and this that thy father may not know it; and this day I will deliver thy brother Abel into thine hands. And Satan sware unto Cain that he would do according to his commands. And all these things were done in secret. And Cain said: Truly I am Mahan, the master of this great secret, that I may murder and get gain. Wherefore Cain was called Master Mahan, and he gloried in his wickedness.[20]

We are warned of such secret combinations in the Book of Mormon, which destroyed the Jaredite civilization, the Nephite civilization, and may destroy ours.[21]

> And Cain went into the field, and Cain talked with Abel, his brother. And it came to pass that while they were in the field, Cain rose up against Abel, his brother, and slew him. And Cain gloried in that which he had done, saying: I am free; surely the flocks of my brother falleth into my hands.[22]

What great advantage would Cain have in gaining his brother's flocks if there were so very few people compared to the apparent number of animals? Again, this part of the story suggests that it is told against a matrix of a much larger population, in a well-established agrarian society.

> And the Lord said unto Cain: Where is Abel, thy brother? And he said: I know not. Am I my brother's keeper? And the Lord said: What hast thou done? The voice of thy brother's blood cries unto me from the ground. And now thou shalt be cursed from the earth which hath opened her mouth to receive thy brother's blood from thy hand. When thou tillest the ground it shall not henceforth yield unto thee her strength. A fugitive and a vagabond shalt thou be in the earth.[23]
>
> And Cain said unto the Lord: Satan tempted me because of my brother's flocks. And I was wroth also; for his offering thou didst accept and not mine; my punishment is greater than I can bear. Behold thou hast driven me out this day from the face of the Lord, and from thy

> face shall I be hid; and I shall be a fugitive and a vagabond in the earth; and it shall come to pass, that he that findeth me will slay me, because of mine iniquities, for these things are not hid from the Lord. And I the Lord said unto him: Whosoever slayeth thee, vengeance shall be taken on him sevenfold. And I the Lord set a mark upon Cain, lest any finding him should kill him.[24]

It may be reasonable here to ask: Who was the "every one" referred to by Cain when he said that his punishment was greater than he could bear? If this story is about one large family, the children of Adam and Eve, who would not know Cain? Why should he be given a distinguishing mark? According to the Genesis account, the only "others" on earth at the time would be his brothers and sisters, and maybe (from the account in Moses) nephews and nieces. Wouldn't his brothers and sisters, nieces and nephews already know him? And why would Cain be a "fugitive and vagabond" when the entire earth was open to one small family? Weren't they all "fugitives and vagabonds"? The next verse suggests that although Adam and Eve were only hearing God's voice from the Garden of Eden,[25] in some way, the family was still in His presence.

> And Cain was shut out from the presence of the Lord, and with his wife and many of his brethren dwelt in the land of Nod, on the east of Eden. And Cain knew his wife, and she conceived and bare Enoch, and he also begat many sons and daughters. And he builded a city, and he called the name of the city after the name of his son, Enoch.[26]

This scripture, to me, is the most compelling that Adam's family was not living in isolation. The "land of Nod" must have been significant at some point in the retelling of the story, but it has little or no meaning today. *Nod* is a Hebrew root word (דונ) comprising the verb (דודנל) meaning "to wander."[27] Therefore, to dwell in Nod simply means that Cain and his family wandered; they were in the "land of wandering." And then Cain built a *city*. The original Hebrew word (הָיְרִק) means "town" or "city."[27] With his wandering family, only a tiny population on the entire face of the earth, why wouldn't Cain have built a village or hamlet? Doesn't it take quite a few people to found a city, or even a town? Cain's fear that someone might kill him, the mark so that people seeing him wouldn't kill him, and his founding a city with his wife and son all suggest that Adam's family was embedded in a society of people already extant when

Adam and Eve left the Garden and not descended only from Adam and Eve—and likely of a sizable number.

And then there is this rather odd statement in the Doctrine and Covenants: "And the Lord administered comfort unto Adam, and said unto him: I have set thee to be at the head; a multitude of nations shall come of thee, and thou art a prince over them forever."[28]

"*A* multitude of nations"? Why would God refer to "a multitude" if *every* nation was descended from him? Furthermore, the story of Enoch, Adam's fourth great grandson, tells us that by his day there were many people in the world from many lands.

> And there came a man unto him [Enoch], whose name was Mahijah, and said unto him: Tell us plainly who thou art, and from whence thou comest? And he said unto them: I came out from the land of Cainan, the land of my fathers, a land of righteousness unto this day. And my father taught me in all the ways of God.[29]

Enoch told Mahijah that he came from "the land of Cainan, the land of my fathers, a land of righteousness unto this day." Why would Mahijah not know of the land of Cainan? Did he not know about Adam? Why would Enoch refer to the land of *my* fathers—not the land of *our* fathers? Enoch then told Mahijah that he was sent by God, who is "my God, and your God, and ye are my brethren."[30] Again, this discussion makes it appear that there were many people on Earth, some of whom knew not Cainan, or Adam, or God. One possibility is that after several generations of godlessness, many descendants may not have known either God or Adam. Another possibility is that there were other people on Earth in addition to Adam's immediate descendants.

Cain's fourth great grandson, Lamech, continued Cain's covenant with Satan and God's curse.

> For Lamech having entered into a covenant with Satan, after the manner of Cain, wherein he became Master Mahan, master of that great secret which was administered unto Cain by Satan; and Irad, the son of Enoch, having known their secret, began to reveal it unto the sons of Adam; Wherefore Lamech, being angry, slew him, not like unto Cain, his brother Abel, for the sake of getting gain, but he slew him for the oath's sake. For, from the days of Cain, there was a secret combination, and their works were in the dark, and they knew every man

> his brother. Wherefore the Lord cursed Lamech, and his house, and all them that had covenanted with Satan; for they kept not the commandments of God, and it displeased God, and he ministered not unto them, and their works were abominations, and began to spread among all the sons of men. And it was among the sons of men.[31]
>
> And among the daughters of men these things were not spoken, because that Lamech had spoken the secret unto his wives, and they rebelled against him, and declared these things abroad, and had not compassion; Wherefore Lamech was despised, and cast out, and came not among the sons of men, lest he should die. And thus the works of darkness began to prevail among all the sons of men.[32]
>
> And God cursed the earth with a sore curse, and was angry with the wicked, with all the sons of men whom he had made; For they would not hearken unto his voice, nor believe on his Only Begotten Son, even him whom he declared should come in the meridian of time, who was prepared from before the foundation of the world.[33]

And, so, from early on, there was a division among the children of Adam between those who followed Satan and those who followed God and Jesus Christ.

> And thus the Gospel began to be preached, from the beginning, being declared by holy angels sent forth from the presence of God, and by his own voice, and by the gift of the Holy Ghost. And thus all things were confirmed unto Adam, by an holy ordinance, and the Gospel preached, and a decree sent forth, that it should be in the world, until the end thereof; and thus it was. Amen.[34]

NOTES

1. Genesis 5:13
2. Moses 4:6
3. Colin McEvedy and Richard Jones, *Atlas of World Population History* (London: Puffin, London, 1978).
4. Moses 5:14–15
5. Moses 6:51–65
6. Galatians 3:29
7. Moses 5:16
8. Mosiah 3:19
9. Helaman 12:1, 4–5
10. Moses 5:17
11. Moses 5:5, 7

12. Moses 5:18–23
13. 2 Nephi 9:9
14. See Doctrine and Covenants 64:15–17.
15. Hugh Nibley, "A Strange Thing in the Land," *Ensign*, 1976.
16. Moses 5:24–25
17. 1 Nephi 8:36
18. Moses 5:26–27
19. Moses 5:28
20. Moses 5:29–31
21. Ether 8:18–19, 22–24
22. Moses 5:32–33
23. Moses 5:34–37
24. Moses 5:38–40
25. Moses 5:4
26. Moses 5:41–42
27. Isaac Asimov, *Asimov's Guide to the Bible : the Old and New Testaments*, (Reprint [der Ausg.] in 2 vol. 1968–1969. ed.) (New York: Wings Books, 1981).
28. Doctrine and Covenants 107:55
29. Moses 6:40–41
30. Moses 6:43
31. Moses 5:49–52
32. Moses 5:53–55
33. Moses 5:56–57
34. Moses 5:58–59

CHAPTER 18

HOW THE INFINITE FALL AFFECTS US

We are told in Moses 5 that Adam was taught the great plan of salvation and Christ's Atonement, as the key to that plan.

> And after many days an angel of the Lord appeared unto Adam, saying: Why dost thou offer sacrifices unto the Lord? And Adam said unto him: I know not, save the Lord commanded me. And then the angel spake, saying: This thing is a similitude of the sacrifice of the Only Begotten of the Father, which is full of grace and truth. Wherefore, thou shalt do all that thou doest in the name of the Son, and thou shalt repent and call upon God in the name of the Son forevermore. And in that day the Holy Ghost fell upon Adam, which beareth record of the Father and the Son, saying: I am the Only Begotten of the Father from the beginning, henceforth and forever, that as thou hast fallen thou mayest be redeemed, and all mankind, even as many as will.[1]

All scripture testifies of Jesus Christ. This revelation to Adam was the first. All the Old Testament scriptures giving minute, drawn-out details of how to perform sacrifice constantly foretold and reminded the Israelites of Christ's Atonement. However, most Israelites, especially the priests, focused more on the minutia of sacrifice than on the Christ, of whom they were a type. Likewise the sacrament today reminds us weekly of the Savior's atonement. Adam and Eve were thrilled with the explanation of the Atonement:

> And in that day Adam blessed God and was filled, and began to prophesy concerning all the families of the earth, saying: Blessed be the name of God, for because of my transgression my eyes are opened, and in this life I shall have joy, and again in the flesh I shall see God. And Eve, his wife, heard all these things and was glad, saying: Were it not for our transgression we never should have had seed, and never should have known good and evil, and the joy of our redemption, and the eternal life which God giveth unto all the obedient.[2]

In further anticipation of the Savior's Atonement, Adam was baptized, and presumably, so too were as many of his family members as would believe and follow their parents' example. Although Eve's baptism is not mentioned in scripture, it is unquestionable that she was baptized shortly after Adam—presumably by Adam himself.

Approximately five hundred fifty years before the birth of the Savior, the prophet Nephi saw the Savior's baptism: "Wherefore, I would that ye should remember that I have spoken unto you concerning that prophet which the Lord showed unto me, that should baptize the Lamb of God, which should take away the sins of the world."[3]

Nephi spoke of this baptism of Christ, more than five hundred years in the future, as though it had already occurred,

> And now, if the Lamb of God, he being holy, should have need to be baptized by water, to fulfil all righteousness, O then, how much more need have we, being unholy, to be baptized, yea, even by water! And now, I would ask of you, my beloved brethren, wherein the Lamb of God did fulfil all righteousness in being baptized by water? Know ye not that he was holy? But notwithstanding he being holy, he showeth unto the children of men that, according to the flesh he humbleth himself before the Father, and witnesseth unto the Father that he would be obedient unto him in keeping his commandments. Wherefore, after he was baptized with water the Holy Ghost descended upon him in the form of a dove. And again, it showeth unto the children of men the straitness of the path, and the narrowness of the gate, by which they should enter, he having set the example before them. And he said unto the children of men: Follow thou me. Wherefore, my beloved brethren, can we follow Jesus save we shall be willing to keep the commandments of the Father? And the Father said: Repent ye, repent ye, and be baptized in the name of my Beloved Son. And also, the voice of the Son came

> unto me, saying: He that is baptized in my name, to him will the Father give the Holy Ghost, like unto me; wherefore, follow me, and do the things which ye have seen me do.[4]

Nephi stated that Jesus "*did* fulfil," "*was* baptized," and "*said* unto the children of men" (all past tense), not that He *will* fulfil, *will* be *baptized*, and *will* say. Nephi was speaking as though the Atonement had already happened, half a millennium before it actually occurred.

Nephi continued his discussion of baptism:

> Wherefore, do the things which I have told you I have seen that your Lord and your Redeemer should do; for, for this cause have they been shown unto me, that ye might know the gate by which ye should enter. For the gate by which ye should enter is repentance and baptism by water; and then cometh a remission of your sins by fire and by the Holy Ghost. And then are ye in this strait and narrow path which leads to eternal life; yea, ye have entered in by the gate; ye have done according to the commandments of the Father and the Son; and ye have received the Holy Ghost, which witnesses of the Father and the Son, unto the fulfilling of the promise which he hath made, that if ye entered in by the way ye should receive.[5]

How do *we* obtain the remission of *our* sins? Through the Atonement of Jesus Christ, and through the shedding of His blood.[6] How do *we* obtain eternal life? Through the mercy of our Lord Jesus Christ.[7] And what is His mercy? The Atonement. Nephi was teaching his people that they could obtain a remission of their sins and eternal life, through the Atonement of Jesus Christ, half a millennium before that Atonement actually occurred. Why? Because the Atonement was "unto the fulfilling of the promise which he hath made."[8] And when was that promise made? It was made in the grand council in heaven, before the foundations of the world. Because we agreed to the great plan of our Eternal Father, we became partakers in its blessings of remission of sins and eternal life, through the promise of the Savior of the World—even *before* the Atonement occurred.

The Atonement was a *fait accompli* long before it actually happened (as long as Christ stayed the course and fulfilled His foreordained mission). The effect of the Atonement could be felt as soon as we accepted it in our premortal lives. Furthermore, we are taught in Mosiah 18 that Nephi's words were not just theoretical, but they were put into practice by the followers of Alma at the Waters of Mormon.

> And it came to pass that he said unto them: Behold, here are the waters of Mormon (for thus were they called) and now, as ye are desirous to come into the fold of God, and to be called his people, and are willing to bear one another's burdens, that they may be light; Yea, and are willing to mourn with those that mourn; yea, and comfort those that stand in need of comfort, and to stand as witnesses of God at all times and in all things, and in all places that ye may be in, even until death, that ye may be redeemed of God, and be numbered with those of the first resurrection, that ye may have eternal life—Now I say unto you, if this be the desire of your hearts, what have you against being baptized in the name of the Lord, as a witness before him that ye have entered into a covenant with him, that ye will serve him and keep his commandments, that he may pour out his Spirit more abundantly upon you? And now when the people had heard these words, they clapped their hands for joy, and exclaimed: This is the desire of our hearts. And now it came to pass that Alma took Helam, he being one of the first, and went and stood forth in the water, and cried, saying: O Lord, pour out thy Spirit upon thy servant, that he may do this work with holiness of heart. And when he had said these words, the Spirit of the Lord was upon him, and he said: Helam, I baptize thee, having authority from the Almighty God, as a testimony that ye have entered into a covenant to serve him until you are dead as to the mortal body; and may the Spirit of the Lord be poured out upon you; and may he grant unto you eternal life, through the redemption of Christ, whom he has prepared from the foundation of the world. And after Alma had said these words, both Alma and Helam were buried in the water; and they arose and came forth out of the water rejoicing, being filled with the Spirit.[9]

Why could the redemption of Jesus Christ be effective over five hundred years before the Atonement? Because the Atonement is infinite. In addition to our acceptance of the plan before the foundations of the world, we are told that there is no time with God:

> Listen to the voice of the Lord your God, even Alpha and Omega, the beginning and the end, whose course is one eternal round, the same today as yesterday, and forever.[10]
>
> For he that diligently seeketh shall find; and the mysteries of God shall be unfolded unto them, by the power of the Holy Ghost, as well in these times as in times of old, and as well in times of old as in times to come; wherefore, the course of the Lord is one eternal round.[11]

Because of the infinite nature of the Atonement, it does not matter when a person is baptized. It does not matter whether baptism occurs before the Atonement, beginning with our father, Adam, or after the Atonement, because with God it is all the same "in these times as in times of old, and as well in times of old as in times to come."[11]

We are told of Adam's baptism in great poetic detail in Moses 6:

> And it came to pass, when the Lord had spoken with Adam, our father, that Adam cried unto the Lord, and he was caught away by the Spirit of the Lord, and was carried down into the water, and was laid under the water, and was brought forth out of the water. And thus he was baptized, and the Spirit of God descended upon him, and thus he was born of the Spirit, and became quickened in the inner man. And he heard a voice out of heaven, saying: Thou art baptized with fire, and with the Holy Ghost. This is the record of the Father, and the Son, from henceforth and forever; And thou art after the order of him who was without beginning of days or end of years, from all eternity to all eternity. Behold, thou art one in me, a son of God; and thus may all become my sons. Amen.[12]

Like Nephi and Alma in the Book of Mormon, Adam was baptized and had the Spirit of God descend upon him long before the Atonement, which would affect the fulfillment of the promise that all may become the sons and daughters of God through baptism. As with Nephi and Alma, it made no difference when Adam was baptized. He did not have to wait until after Christ's Atonement was actually fulfilled for two reasons: First, we all agreed to the plan of the atonement and baptism before the foundations of the earth, and second, time is irrelevant to God. All things are before God and with Him there is no time.

> Lord, thou hast been our dwelling place in all generations. Before the mountains were brought forth, or ever thou hadst formed the earth and the world, even from everlasting to everlasting, thou art God. Thou turnest man to destruction; and sayest, Return, ye children of men. For a thousand years in thy sight are but as yesterday when it is past, and as a watch in the night. Thou carriest them away as with a flood; they are as a sleep: in the morning they are like grass which groweth up.[13]
>
> Thy throne is established of old: thou art from everlasting.[14]
>
> But thou, O Lord, shalt endure for ever; and thy remembrance unto all generations.[15]
>
> I said, O my God, take me not away in the midst of my days: thy years are throughout all generations. Of old hast thou laid the

> foundation of the earth: and the heavens are the work of thy hands. They shall perish, but thou shalt endure: yea, all of them shall wax old like a garment; as a vesture shalt thou change them, and they shall be changed: But thou art the same, and thy years shall have no end.[16]
>
> But, beloved, be not ignorant of this one thing, that one day is with the Lord as a thousand years, and a thousand years as one day.[17]

Along with the account of Adam's baptism, there is also a hint of his ordination to the priesthood: "And thou art after the order of him who was without beginning of days or end of years, from all eternity to all eternity."[18]

The Doctrine and Covenants leaves no doubt that Adam was a high priest: "Three years previous to the death of Adam, he called Seth, Enos, Cai nan, Mahalaleel, Jared, Enoch, and Methuselah, who were all high priests, with the residue of his posterity who were righteous, into the valley of Adam-ondi-Ahman, and there bestowed upon them his last blessing."[19]

Terryl and Fiona Givens shared the beautiful teaching of the Prophet Joseph Smith concerning these ordinances:

> God not only revealed all the ordinances of salvation to Adam, Joseph [Smith] taught, but intended them "to be the same forever, and set Adam to watch over them [and] to reveal them from heaven to man or send Angels to reveal them 'in the event of their loss." Their unvarying employment was the token of a covenant that binds us to premortal conventions we participated in creating; they constitute "the most perfect order and harmony—and their limits and bounds were fixed irrevocably and voluntarily subscribed to."[20]

The Atonement of Jesus Christ was an infinite and eternal atonement, established before the foundations of the world. That Atonement was in place to return us to the presence of God, even before we left that presence, and which we left because of the infinite fall, which also was established before the foundations of the world. As with all those who participated in baptism long before the atonement actually occurred, likewise the numerous people born before the Fall of Adam and Eve, were born into the fallen world and left God's presence because of the infinite and eternal nature of the fall, even though, for them, it had not yet occurred.

NOTES

1. Moses 5:6–9
2. Moses 5:10–11
3. 2 Nephi 31:4
4. 2 Nephi 31:5–12
5. 2 Nephi 31:17–18
6. Doctrine and Covenants 27:2
7. Jude 1:21
8. 2 Nephi 31:18
9. Mosiah 18:8–14
10. Doctrine and Covenants 35:1
11. 1 Nephi 10:19
12. Moses 6:64–68
13. Psalm 90:1–5
14. Psalm 93:2
15. Psalm 102:12
16. Psalm 102:24–27
17. 2 Peter 3:8
18. Moses 6:67
19. Doctrine and Covenants 107:53
20. Terryl and Fiona Givens, *The Crucible of Doubt* (Salt Lake City: Deseret Book, 2014), 48; citing Robert B. Thompson, Oct. 5, 1840, in Andrew F. Ehat and Lyndon W. Cook, eds., *The Words of Joseph Smith: The Contemporary Accounts of the Nauvoo Discourses of the Prophet Joseph* Smith (Orem, Utah: Grandin, 1994), 39; and citing *Times and Seasons* 4, September 15, 1843: 331

ABOUT THE AUTHOR

Trent D. Stephens, PhD, is an emeritus professor of anatomy and embryology at Idaho State University. He holds BS degrees in microbiology and zoology from Brigham Young University, an MS in zoology from BYU, and a PhD in anatomy from the University of Pennsylvania. He completed postdoctoral training in pediatrics at the University of Washington and has been teaching anatomy and embryology at Idaho State University since 1981.

He was selected as the ISU Distinguished Teacher in 1992 and Outstanding Researcher in 2000. He has published more than one hundred scientific papers and books, and is considered one of the world's leading authorities on the birth defects caused by the drug thalidomide. He has authored *The Infinite Creation* and *Atlas of Human Embryology*, and has coauthored fifteen textbooks of anatomy and physiology.

Trent has held many leadership positions in The Church of Jesus Christ of Latter-day Saints. He and his wife, Kathleen, have served for many years as temple workers in the Idaho Falls Temple. They are the parents of five children and fourteen grandchildren. Their youngest son, Sergeant Blake Christopher Stephens, was killed in Iraq in 2007.